THE WAR ON
CHRISTMAS

THE WAR ON CHRISTMAS

HOW THE LIBERAL PLOT TO BAN
THE SACRED CHRISTIAN HOLIDAY IS
WORSE THAN YOU THOUGHT

JOHN GIBSON

SENTINEL

SENTINEL
Published by the Penguin Group
Penguin Group (USA) Inc., 375 Hudson Street,
New York, New York 10014, U.S.A.
Penguin Group (Canada), 90 Eglinton Avenue East, Suite 700,
Toronto, Ontario, Canada M4P 2Y3
(a division of Pearson Penguin Canada Inc.)
Penguin Books Ltd, 80 Strand, London WC2R 0RL, England
Penguin Ireland, 25 St. Stephen's Green, Dublin 2, Ireland
(a division of Penguin Books Ltd)
Penguin Books Australia Ltd, 250 Camberwell Road, Camberwell,
Victoria 3124, Australia
(a division of Pearson Australia Group Pty Ltd)
Penguin Books India Pvt Ltd, 11 Community Centre, Panchsheel Park,
New Delhi – 110 017, India
Penguin Group (NZ), Cnr Airborne and Rosedale Roads, Albany,
Auckland 1310, New Zealand
(a division of Pearson New Zealand Ltd)
Penguin Books (South Africa) (Pty) Ltd, 24 Sturdee Avenue,
Rosebank, Johannesburg 2196, South Africa

Penguin Books Ltd, Registered Offices:
80 Strand, London WC2R 0RL, England

First published in 2005 by Sentinel,
a member of Penguin Group (USA) Inc.

ISBN 1-59523-016-5

Printed in the United States of America
Set in Adobe Garamond with ATHandle Oldstyle
Designed by Daniel Lagin

For my wife, Susan,
my grandchildren, John and Faith,
and their parents, Jake and Sheri.

PREFACE

Christmas was in the air, and the four-year-old's father noticed the seasonal artwork from preschool piling up on the kitchen table. Among the wrinkled watercolor paintings from art class were sheets of paper bearing clearly recognizable images. On one sheet his son had painted a menorah, and on another, seven candles painted red, green, and black.

The father asked his son about the menorah and the boy answered accurately, if not completely, that it involved a miracle. The father nodded his approval. As for the red and black and green candles the boy said it was Kwanzaa. The father thought there ought to be a painting of a Christmas tree if his son were painting menorahs and Kwanzaa candles. But his son had painted no watercolors of a Christmas tree.

His small son had already asked his mother why the family didn't have a menorah. "Because we're not Jewish, honey, we're Christian," she had replied.

But it bothered the father. Why did my son think we should have a menorah? And why was there no watercolor painting of a Christmas tree among his preschool artwork?

The father had been looking forward to a picture of a Christmas tree from art class to teach his son how to spell the word Christmas. But instead of teaching his son a lesson, the father got a bracing and memorable lesson himself. The boy's father recounted the story for me.

"'Did you draw a Christmas tree?' I asked my son, expecting to hear that he had, and that he had learned about the Christmas tree and the day we celebrate the birth of Jesus," he said. "Instead my son looked up at me and said, 'We have the friendship tree.' I was stunned. I asked him, 'What is a friendship tree?' He just shrugged and said people should be friends.

"With a little more probing I realized no one at the school had taught him about a Christmas tree. They had renamed it. Now, as far as my son and thirty other kids were concerned, it was not the Christmas tree, it was the friendship tree. They had taken the Christmas tree away from my son, even though it wasn't theirs to take."

This father decided to see what was going on in the school, so the next day he made a point of taking his boy to class.

Upon entering the school the next morning, he saw hallway bulletin boards decorated with menorahs and big block letters spelling out HAPPY HANUKAH. Farther down the hall he found the red and black and green candles and letters announcing THE MIRACLE OF KWANZAA. At the end of a long hallway was a small pine tree on a table, which, despite its complete lack of decoration, most people would recognize as a Christmas tree.

The father asked the principal, "What is that tree down the hall?"

The principal beamed proudly. "That is our friendship tree."

"Why don't you call it what it is: a Christmas Tree?" the father asked.

"Oh, we're trying to make sure we don't offend people. It's better to call it a 'friendship tree,'" the principal replied.

Thinking back on the incident a few months later, the father took a grim satisfaction that he had changed the outlook of the principal of this expensive private school in the New York City suburbs. But not by argument or persuasion. "I told him if that tree wasn't a Christmas tree tomorrow, I would be taking my son out of the school, and I would be making certain the other parents I know, who also pay tens of thousands of dollars to the school, would learn how their children were being taught incorrectly. We all know what a Christmas tree is, and I want my son to know what a Christmas tree is. I have no idea what a friendship tree is and I'm damn certain that principal didn't either. It was all about putting Christmas down."

ACKNOWLEDGMENTS

The author would like to thank his editor, Bernadette Malone, of Sentinel for her counsel and direction; his agent, Mel Berger of the William Morris Agency for his patience and judgment; and Scott Norvell of Fox News, who also runs TongueTied, a Web site that tracks the annual parade of Christmas outrages.

In addition, he would like to acknowledge the invaluable assistance of Jake Gibson, who secured documents and conducted interviews; Caroline Sprinkel, who arranged for interviews with various people quoted in this book; Barbara Gray, who researched facts; and Transcript Associates, where transcribers toiled into the night to make certain he received transcribed interviews on time.

He would also like to thank Roger Ailes of Fox News for his invaluable guidance.

CONTENTS

INTRODUCTION

CNN anchor Aaron Brown was giving a speech to the University of Washington in April 2005, when he veered off into a digression that had evidently been gnawing at him for some time.

"[Fox News Channel's Bill] O'Reilly did about two weeks on taking the Christ out of Christmas. Who the hell is worrying about that?"

The audience, liberal college students, laughed and applauded loudly, which was the response Brown undoubtedly wanted.

Aaron Brown may have demonstrated a certain fashionable hipness, a Jon Stewart ironic sneer that would please a predictably liberal college audience gathered to hear a CNN anchor, but in doing so he demonstrated how disconnected he is from millions and millions of Americans who feel that Christmas is under attack in such a sustained and strategized manner that there is, no doubt, a *war* on Christmas. It's no longer permissible to wish anyone Merry Christmas. That's too exclusive, too insensitive. What if they're not Christian? What if they're an atheist? A school in Maryland is now questioning Thanksgiving because, after all, to whom are we giving thanks if not to God, and we all know we can't have that in the public schools.

You might assume that this war is being fought in blue states, bastions of liberalism and multiculturalism, where anything traditional, Christian, or Western is a target. But the war on Christmas is broader than you can imagine. All across America the battle is being joined. As you will read in these pages, Christmas is under attack in bright red states such as Oklahoma, Georgia, Texas, and Indiana.

You might think that the war on Christmas is being fought on the grounds that overtly religious symbols in public—such as nativity scenes and crosses—violate the separation of church and state that many judges have read into the First Amendment of the U.S. Constitution.

But again, you'd be underestimating the war on Christmas. It's worse than you think. Liberals' attacks now focus on symbols regarded by most Americans—and even by the Supreme Court of the United States (in its *Lynch v. Donnelly* ruling) to be secular symbols of the federal holiday that is Christmas. Wannabe constitutional lawyers in local government offices all over the country are declaring unconstitutional normal and traditional Christmas representations such as Christmas trees, Santa Claus, treetop stars, wreaths, the singing of and listening to Christmas carols or Christmas instrumental music, attending a performance of Dickens's *A Christmas Carol,* the publication of the word "Christmas" itself, and even the colors red and green!

Furthermore, the war on Christmas is not just a loopy American preoccupation with lawsuits. This book may focus only on the domestic front, because that is my beat as a television news anchor, but the same phenomenon is afoot in Great Britain, Australia, and most of Europe as well. As an illustration of the problem, here is a sobering letter that arrived last Christmas on the desk of an editor of the *Times* of London:

Sir,

As many as 80,000 Brits (as well as a huge number of others from non-Islamic nations) live in the United Arab Emirates, where the country's indigenous people live by Sharia (Islamic law). Yet shopping centres are decorated with Christmas finery, stores pipe Christmas tunes to every corner, malls are full of children of all nationalities excitedly queueing to see Santa, and advertisements are fully geared to everything Christmas-related . . . a bit like it used to be in the UK before political correctness crept in.

Hotels hold tree-lighting ceremonies and carol services by swimming pools, and holidaymakers stand amazed when Santa rides into town on a camel, handing out gifts.

I have heard of no local being offended by any of these supposed insults and no one complains of being singled out for persecution.

Bah humbug to the ignorant council killjoys who obviously have no understanding of what it really means to have a faith; we in the UAE are having a very happy Christmas, thank you.

Faithfully,
Chris Moran,
Dubai Country Club,
Dubai, United Arab Emirates.

In Dubai and elsewhere in the Muslim world it's all the Christmas you want, out in the open for all to see, enjoy, or ignore. But in officially Christian Great Britain (the Church of England) Christmas is under siege from people whose faith is political correctness and a massive influx of Muslim immigrants. In Birmingham, England, Christmas has become Winterval, an acceptable alternative to non-Christians (Muslims and Jews, primarily). But what a hollow substitute for Christmas!

In the United States of America, a nation overwhelmingly Christian (authoritative polling figures range from 72 percent to 84 percent), literally any sign of Christmas in public can lead to complaints, litigation, angry protest, threats, and bruised feelings. And every year we are treated to the sight of more limitations placed on Christmas.

In December 2004, Pasco county officials in Port Richey, Florida, banned Christmas trees placed in public areas of the county administration building. (The ban was rescinded two days later, after a public outcry.) And in King County, Washington, library administrators banned Christmas trees from the libraries in November 2004, explaining they didn't want to be insensitive to patrons who don't celebrate Christmas. They, too, rescinded the policy in a storm of protest. "We heard from the feedback that Christmas trees are a cultural symbol, not necessarily a religious symbol," said a chastened library official.

But often the Christmas bashers get away with it. (Some muggers get away with it too.)

When the Kensington, Maryland, town council voted in 2004 to purge Santa Claus from its thirty-year-old tradition of lighting a pine tree in front of town hall (because, said the mayor, "two families felt that they would be uncomfortable with Santa Claus being a part of the event") the order stuck. Equally unfair, when in 2004 a New Hampshire junior high school student dressed in a Santa suit was told he was not welcome because the dance was a holiday dance and not a Christmas dance, the order stuck.

Residents of La Jolla, California, who objected to a proposal before the town council to change the name of the Christmas parade to holiday parade in 2004 were labeled anti-Semites by someone who wanted the town's parade to be more "inclusive." And the mayor of Somerville, Massachusetts, apologized after a news release mistakenly referred to the December 21, city-sponsored holiday party as a Christmas party in 2004.

Often the first shots of the battle are fired in schools. Many schools have either already changed Christmas trees into friendship trees or giving trees or holiday trees, or are considering it. Almost everywhere a school district is limiting what Christmas carols kids can sing or hear, or a district is considering it. Almost everywhere a school district has decided that kids cannot have Christmas parties, but instead must have winter parties; almost everywhere school administrators have either disinvited Santa or are giving him sidelong glances of suspicion, and in some schools the winter theme must be so completely universal that even the colors red and green are forbidden.

Whose fault is this? Well, for those who like to jump to conclusions, no, it's not just liberal Jews. I should state for the record that my Jewish son helped me research this book because he agrees that the war on Christmas has gone too far. The large number of foot soldiers waging the war on Christmas is in fact made up mostly of liberal white Christians, some of whom may have Jewish-sounding names (Cohen, Horoschak) that could mislead readers to a dangerous and very unfair conclusion. So let's restate for the record: The wagers of this war on Christmas are a cabal of secularists, so-called humanists, trial lawyers, cultural relativists, and liberal, guilt-wracked Christians—not just Jewish people. Muslims have spent their energies so far fighting for rights and against discrimination and are not big players in the anti-Christian movement.

Providing the legal muscle and pretzel logic to the anti-Christmas warriors are brand-name liberal institutions such as the American Civil Liberties Union (ACLU), the Anti-Defamation League of the B'nai Brith (ADL), and the Americans for the Separation of Church and State (ASCS). Some institutional backers of the war on Christmas are Christian churches, such as the Unitarians and the United Church of Christ who celebrate Jesus Christ's humanity and leave the room when the discussion turns to his divinity. These are the churches that marry gays and turn their backs on preborn babies. Their congregants vote for John Kerry, Ted Kennedy, and Barney Frank. They are liberal by definition, and they proclaim their liberal values; I began to connect the dots and discerned the outlines of the conspiracy.

The plot to ban Christmas itself is anything but secret. It is embedded in the secular "Humanist Manifesto" (in its three iterations from the American Humanist Association) in the philosophy of teaching of John Dewey, in the legal opinions of Laurence Tribe, in the rulings of the Ninth Circuit Court of Appeal on which sits the most liberal jurist in the land, Stephen Reinhardt, who is married to Ramona Ripston, the southern California ACLU executive director and the national group's most liberal and effective leader.

These are the people who fly over the masses they seek to dictate to, crisscrossing the country back and forth from Hollywood to New York City, who attend each other's dinner parties and lament the Christian conservatives, who are certain that the people who voted for George Bush want to install a Christian Taliban as custodians of the levers of power.

These are the groups that actively threaten any public official who dares put Christmas (and therefore Christianity) in a public place. The threats are delivered in the form of a letter objecting to a public Christmas display, but they soon morph into a lawsuit demanding the defendant (the school district, city, county) not only banish the public Christmas images but pay the legal expenses of the group bringing the lawsuit. What cash-strapped school official can afford to waste precious pennies paying the court fees of a skilled ACLU lawyer if they defeat the small town in court before a liberal judge? More than one school official has described these tactics as "intimidation" and "blackmail."

These liberal groups give lip service to religion, but only as a completely personal activity that should be practiced and celebrated behind the closed doors of privately held property (evidently it would be preferred they were in windowless and soundproof rooms, lest some expression of religion escape into the air breathed by others). The trail of evidence has led me to wonder whether their problem is Christmas or Christianity itself. Often, Christianity itself is the target of their prohibitions. Expressions of Judaism and Islam and Hinduism are regarded as inoffensive and merely cultural, but any expression of Christianity is, in their eyes, entirely religious and devoid of the cultural safeguards that would permit its presence in public society.

If symbols of Christianity need banning, in their minds Christmas itself needs banning, too.

And if Christmas is to be banned, then an overwhelming majority of Americans are denied Christmas in public places.

Part of the reason I wrote this book was my experience as a Fox
News Channel anchor during Christmas 2004. The channel's
chairman, Roger Ailes, decided to put station identification breaks
on the air in which Fox wished viewers Merry Christmas.

You could almost hear the collective gasp in the public. Look!
A television network is putting the words "Merry Christmas" on
the air! (Ailes also put "Happy Hanukah" on the air.)

"The most disturbing letter I got during the whole Christmas
season," Ailes told me, "was a letter that said, 'You must be a very
brave man.'

"Now why would I be a 'brave man' for saying Merry Christmas?" Ailes asked.

I was also bothered by what I saw going on. I was raised outside the church by a mother who was raised in a convent. I was
kept at a distance, but I was always taught to respect people's religious practices, and not to harbor malevolent suspicions about
those who felt the call to praise the lord and spread the word. The
ones who make me more uncomfortable are those who mock,
disparage, and denigrate religion and the religious. Their thinly
veiled hostility gives me the creeps—not evangelical Christians!

I grew up in far northern California, in the shadow of Mount
Shasta around people who were Catholics, Baptists, Nazarenes,
Pentecostals, Jehovah's Witnesses, Assembly of God witnesses. All
are required by the tenets of their faith to spread the word of Jesus Christ and his disciples. All exercised their right of free speech
to say what they were called to say about God. Even if I were put
off by their passion, I knew their right to speak required my tol-

erance, my ability to admit to myself their speech did me no harm.

I have never been kidnapped and packed off to a church. No one has ever threatened me for not responding to their pleadings for me to attend.

After all these years watching Christmas come and go, and watching the courts rule on church and state issues—sometimes sensibly, sometimes not—I have seen the equally important right of the free expression of religion whittled away.

Christians have a right to put up a Christmas tree in a school and call it what it is. They shouldn't have to call it a "paradise tree" or a "friendship tree" or a "giving tree" or a "world tree" or a "holiday tree" just because it's in a public place, any more than Jews should have to call a menorah (which represents a religious miracle to them) a "holiday candelabra" in case Christians or atheists are offended.

Are Christians right for wanting their children to be able to sing and hear Christmas carols that may contain religious references? Are those carols expressions of abject religious devotion or can they also be thought of as traditional songs for the season? Are parents right to want to see "Christmas break" on the school calendar instead of the neutered "winter break"? Are they right to want their children to see Dickens's *A Christmas Carol,* the tale of a bitter old man and his Christmas redemption? Are they right to be affronted when a school administrator who has canceled a trip to see *A Christmas Carol* justifies his decision by saying, "We canceled a trip to see *Harry Potter* too," as if the timelessness of Dickens has somehow been trumped by the talented but not yet tested Ms. Rowling?

I think the answers to all these questions are yes.

So what of the others who don't feel included?

As Ben Stein, the financial guru and frequent television guest, said in his book of small sayings that he has used to help himself get through life, "Feelings are not facts."

Feeling excluded is not being excluded. I do not feel excluded because Muslims go on a hajj, or because they observe the fasting of Ramadan in my presence. I do not feel excluded because Jews observe Passover.

In the schools, any appearance of Christianity is treated like a hazmat crisis.

The story of this book, the stunning and shocking revelation contained here, is the perversely widespread war on Christmas that we have all seen in our own personal experiences. It is led by people in charge of municipal governments, corporations, and especially school boards, and by overzealous civil liberties lawyers. They claim they are only adhering to the Constitution, but they have all run far out in front of the Supreme Court of the United States, and far out in front of the First Amendment that carries the promise that 1) "Congress shall make no law respecting an establishment of religion," and 2) "or prohibiting the free exercise thereof." The second clause is just as important as the first, but the liberal cabal out to ban Christmas has trampled it. A free expression of Christmas in this age is fast becoming impossible.

My brother received a Christmas card from one of our cousins, who lives near Redding, California, where we grew up. The image on it made me realize that I am in my late fifties, and that the expressions of Christmas I enjoyed as a boy would today be considered shocking and offensive in many places.

The front of the card was a black-and-white photograph of

downtown Redding taken in the early 1950s, judging from the newest car parked on the street: a clearly identifiable 1953 Buick.

On a clear pre-Christmas day, the photograph shows a close mountain in the background, appearing to be covered in something dark, a shadowed surface that I know to be, undoubtedly, the ubiquitous manzanita bush, a beautiful bush that grows densely, with small light green leaves and twisted branches of a hard, deep red wood. In the foreground of the photograph is the town itself, which is situated at a low elevation that seldom if ever saw snow. The street and sidewalks in the photograph are winter cold and as clean as they would be in summer.

It was the downtown where I grew up, from my earliest memories of ventures outside the home, and had I been seen in this photograph the day it was taken I would have been a skinny red-headed and toothy boy of about seven. It was a downtown of two or three small department stores, a hotel, a Texaco gas station, various small eateries usually called "Coffee Shop," a supply store, and assorted other merchants that would support a town of about twenty thousand people. Close to the camera is the looming faux deco marquee tower of the Cascade movie theater, named after the Cascade Mountains that surround the town. If my guess that the year is 1953 is right, it was evidently not much of a year for Hollywood Christmas blockbusters. The Christmas season attraction at the Cascade was Leo Gorcey in the Bowery Boys's *Angels In Disguise.* Tim Allen's Christmas movie career was still several decades in the future.

What is startling about the photograph is the depiction of Christmas in Redding, California, 1953. The giant face of Santa Claus hangs on a garland of evergreen twisted with strings of lights that stretches across the entire street. More of the same garlands, featuring California mission–style bells and stars and wreaths and Santa's face, stretch down Market Street as far as the lens can see.

At a far distant intersection of a crossing side street and Market Street, blocking the view of anything beyond, is a giant conifer— a pine tree, specifically a sugar pine, I believe—placed in a manhole in the center of the street. The Christmas tree completely towers over everything, much taller than any of the buildings, the tallest of which appears to be three stories. The enormous tree is peaked by a large star that is illuminated brightly at night. After dark the street was blazing with garland lights over the street, and the mighty tree above everything, twinkling with thousands of lights.

I remember this tree very well. You couldn't drive downtown without passing under it, and around it, virtually through it. The trunk was always painted white up to a height of about six feet, in a futile effort to redirect Christmas inebriates and the absentminded from walking or driving into it. The tree always absorbed a car wreck or two, but it was so stout, so tall, the trunk so thick, the inevitable impacts did little more than shake a few lights.

To a small child the tree was evergreen and ever present when your parents took you on a Christmas shopping outing. It was an enormous presence of the Christmas season, a true highlight, as big and as imposing as anything I had ever seen when I was just a boy. People grow up, of course. I have come to see bigger objects and structures, but nothing sticks in my memory like that colossal tree.

Driving slowly under it, other cars passing by at a crawl, the wide-eyed child could see up close and in detail what made it shine so brightly. It was strung with colored lightbulbs that were big and painted bright colors. I remember the lightbulbs as fist size, though I am certain now they were large but conventional 100-watt bulbs. I rode by countless times, under the outstretched boughs of that enormous tree, the lights blazing, the smell of the big pine overpowering, one bug-eyed child out of many in a parade of cars passing under the canopy of enormous branches that seemed to cover an entire intersection of streets.

Redding was a lumber town, and the significance of the tree was not only the statement of a big Christmas; it also said, "This is a town of big trees. We know where to find the biggest of big trees and we can bring one right into the center of town and make it stand upright in the street just as if it were in your living room at home." It was a declaration of both Christmas and the proud industry of the area, lumber.

Oddly, considering the climate of political correctness these days, they still do these things in Redding, California. The 2004 Christmas season was the eighty-fifth year Redding observed this tradition. The newspaper reported that the latest downtown Christmas tree measured eighty-nine feet from base to tip and, though large, it no longer towered over most buildings in town. Redding has progressed and now boasts structures taller than trees.

The 2004 tree came from a small town west of Redding called Shingletown, where for the last thirty-four years a tree has been cut from land now owned by Sierra Pacific Industries. Volunteeers from the local fire departments, the electric company, and logging and trucking companies donated their time and expertise to bring the tree down and truck it to the spot in front of the Redding mall, where it was erected for the season. People who are old enough to remember the tree in the middle of Market Street before the city allowed the construction of a covering over the street, what they call a mall, say today's tree and today's setting (an asphalt expanse next to the mall) have diminished the experience. Nonetheless, both the tree cutting and the tree lighting are still civic traditions that bring out crowds of Christmas season enthusiasts. It is not Rockefeller Center, and not as many people come to see the Redding tree, but it is a proud tradition nonetheless, and it continues without the assistance or interference of lawyers. At least, so far.

All this seems odd to me, because in so many towns and villages and cities in this country the anti-Christmas atmosphere makes Redding the exception, not the rule. (In fact, Redding is planning more Christmas, not less. The Viva Downtown civic booster organization is planning more lighted wreaths on light poles downtown.)

More than fifty years have passed since I first saw Redding's mammoth Christmas tree, and even though the tradition continues, I suspect some of the public statements of Christmas found in the Christmas card photograph of my youth cannot be put on display today. I can't see it in the photograph, but I am quite certain there is a nativity scene somewhere in the shadows of the background. Today that crèche would be retired to a church.

Looking back at the Redding, California, in the photograph of Christmas on Market Street, noticing the Christmas of my youth, the Santa face, the garlands, the stars, the wreaths, the enormous Christmas tree, I realized that the research for this book had shown me that virtually every one of those symbols of Christmas is now under attack as an impermissible public declaration of a religious holiday, the Christian Christmas, and somewhere in this country has been banned.

While it is true that there is no nationwide ban on Santa

Claus, evergreen garlands, Christmas wreaths, treetop stars, jingling bells, and Christmas trees, and that the United States Supreme Court has never ruled that they are forbidden, even on public land, in public buildings, or especially in the public schools, it is also true that in many local communities, in local government offices, and in school board offices these are the new symbols of the separation of church and state. We have moved on from objections to the clearly religious symbol of a nativity scene, and now every one of these formerly secular symbols of Christmas has been banned, forbidden, and disallowed by some satrap of local officialdom, some school superintendent, some city manager, some superior court judge, some possessor of executive fiat somewhere in this country.

Yes, Virginia, there is a war on Christmas. And in the coming chapters you will learn that it's much worse than you dreamed.

THE WAR ON CHRISTMAS

CHAPTER 1

COVINGTON, GEORGIA:

"WE COULDN'T CALL IT CHRISTMAS"

Typically a battle in the war on Christmas begins with a letter from the infamous American Civil Liberties Union (ACLU). So it was in Covington, Georgia, in December 2000, where the Newton County school board received a letter announcing ACLU court action if the school board members followed through with their announced intention to use the word "Christmas" on the school calendar, as they had in the past.

In Covington, Georgia, the fight over religion in the schools had devolved to a single word. Other places debated the crèche, or the Christmas tree, or Christmas carols, but in this small Georgia town the simple word "Christmas" was enough to invite a lawsuit.

In earlier times, Christmas was an entirely unremarkable word, but in the new millennium in American schools it had become a word that was fraught with new meanings and new implications.

If the school calendar contained the word "Christmas" was the school board of Newton County, Georgia, endorsing or supporting the Christian religion? To the school board it was nothing more than correctly identifying the Christmas vacation period, but to the ACLU the mere designation of that particular two-week break from classes in school as a Christmas vacation was an unconstitutional entanglement of church and state.

The school board had seesawed back and forth during the winter months of 2000 trying to decide if the word "Christmas" could be put back on the school calendar. It would simply be a word on a square of the calendar, or a word on a listing of dates school would not be in session. It was a mere reversion to the use of a word abandoned a few years earlier when, in a fit of one-world multiculturalism, the school board had changed the name of the Christmas break to winter break. Now a member of the school board wanted the calendar to go back to Christmas. In some school districts, though not many, the two-week school break had come to be known by the more chancy designation "holiday break," which seems to say there is a holiday that is being celebrated but one the school district is hesitant to actually name.

In Covington, it was just a matter of a word switch, from winter to Christmas. Nothing else would have changed. The holiday break would remain the same, and the reason for the break would remain the same. Schools close for a Christmas break for two reasons: first, a simple recognition that a large number of students will not be sent to school by their parents; and second, the safety issue that a large number of teachers and staff will not come to school, thereby creating a safety hazard for students who do attend. In either case, it is not a recognition or an endorsement of the religious holiday.

The school board member who pushed for the return of Christmas was Richard Tiede. He died in a motorcycle accident in 2004 and can no longer speak for himself, but his widow, Nancy, remembers why he wanted the change back to Christmas. "He felt that there was just too much political correctness going on and people were sidestepping the issues," Nancy Tiede said in an interview with me, recalling her husband's discomfort with the banishment of Christmas from the school calendar. "It was just too . . . too," and here she hesitates, looking for the right word. "It was just too extreme."

Richard Tiede, said his widow, thought the school break simply ought to be called what it is. "The reason that we have a break at that particular time of the year in the school system was because the majority of our students celebrated Christmas and the families like to be together at that time."

Nonetheless, that reality was not important to the ACLU. The word change would have been constitutionally significant to the ACLU and its Atlanta-based lawyer, Craig Goodmark.

Goodmark was freshly out of law school just two years earlier. He graduated from the University of Florida law school and set up shop and life in Atlanta, Georgia. He specialized in education law, and was a volunteer attorney for the local chapter of the ACLU. His practice generally consisted of any matters that came up regarding education policy or programs. "My regular job was to represent teachers from the largest teachers' union in Georgia, the Georgia Association of Educators, in their labor disputes. But through the ACLU I became aware of this case and they asked me if I would get involved. I said, 'Yeah,'" Goodmark said to me in an interview in 2005, five years later. He drove the thirty-odd miles down to Covington to make a stand, and appeared before the Newton County school board, of which Tiede was a member.

"The school board of Newton County had made an affirmative decision," he said, "to change what had been called the 'winter holiday' to the 'Christmas holiday.' And they had made it through an official action of the board, which means that they

did it during a meeting and they did it on the record." For Goodmark it was a straightforward case of entanglement of government (the school board) with religion (Christianity).

"I think they were just saying, We're taking back the holiday
for Christmas. And a group of people called up the ACLU saying
that they were offended by this. That they believed that this excluded them and sent a message to their children who are forced
to go to these public schools that they weren't welcome there."

In his appearance before the schoolboard, Goodmark objected
vehemently, saying the use of the word "Christmas" on the calendar
to describe the December vacation, which usually and normally and
typically is taken so Christians may observe the Christmas holiday,
was, in the ACLU's term, "unconstitutional."

As an observational matter, the school district certainly was
letting schoolchildren out of school during the two weeks of December that included Christmas Day, and no one was confused as
to what the holiday break really was. No one, for instance, believed the holiday was to observe and commemorate winter sol-
stice or saturnalia, the festival of drinking and gorging ancient
pagans celebrated in winter months. Jewish parents of Jewish
schoolchildren certainly knew why their children would not be
required to attend school during those two weeks, as did Hindu
parents, as did Muslim parents (if there were any in Covington,
Georgia, in 2000).

Nonetheless, the ACLU saw a great danger in admitting on
the school calendar exactly why it was that children would not be
attending school for those ten days at the end of December. In
the ACLU's view even acknowledging why schoolchildren were
going to be absent from school and home with their parents—the
Christmas holiday—was not merely an acknowledgment of real-

ity, not merely a descriptive issue of the days in question, but through the use of the one word ("Christmas") constituted an illegal and unconstitutional and entirely impermissible [emphasis added] "*endorsement* of a particular religion."

"We explained that this was establishment of religion in a public or in a government entity and that would be illegal," Goodmark said in our interview. "It would be violative of the First Amendment. It would coerce these children to participate in a Christmas holiday. It would be an affirmative act of the government to prefer one religion over the other, which would be illegal."

In aggressively trying to stamp out any semblance of Christianity in a place it finds Christianity abhorrent (in the presence of schoolchildren) the ACLU was asking people to ignore the obvious, to pretend that they did not know why the school break was taking place.

"To call it a Christmas break would be endorsing one religion over the other, which would be Christianity over other religions or the absence of a religion," Goodmark said in an interview almost five years later. He was a little foggy on exactly what had happened, and had not consulted his notes or letters to the school board before the interview, he told me. Nonetheless, he knew that even saying it was the Christmas season was a constitutional issue. At least, he had convinced himself. "That would be violative of the establishment clause, which says that the government will not endorse or the government will refrain from the establishment of religion."

In this instance, the ACLU was once again straining reality in service to an antireligion or, to be precise, an anti-Christian political agenda. Simply put, there is no law or ruling from the

Supreme Court of the United States that would justify banning the word "Christmas" from the school calendar, and Goodmark's superiors at the Georgia ACLU had to know that. But they also had to know that the Covington, Georgia, school board was not made up of constitutional lawyers and would not have kept up with Supreme Court rulings. Additionally, the school board would probably not be willing to incur the cost of litigating the matter, especially if it were threatened with the possibility of losing and being forced to pay the ACLU litigation costs.

In fact, the board members would not have been forced to spend even a dollar to clear up the matter. They would only have had to place a call or sent an e-mail to the National School Boards Association (NSBA), a national advisory organization.

Tom Hutton, an attorney with the NSBA, would have informed Covington officials, free of charge, that the Christmas break is not an endorsement of Christianity and its holiday, but simply an observance of fact. "When schools observe religious holidays by closing school, the legally acceptable reason they're doing it is, the kids won't be there anyway," Hutton said in an interview. The same reasoning applies when the example is a holiday for Ramadan in largely Muslim Dearborn, Michigan, which has seen a dramatic rise in the population of Arab Muslims in the last two decades. "So it's not that we're forcing Islam on anybody in Dearborn, Michigan, it's that the kids aren't going to be there. And the same with Christmas. We close school on Christmas 'cause the kids aren't going to be there."

Hutton provided the practiced eye for the correct view of the law. Any number of Christian legal groups would have gladly dispatched the lawyers.

The question would eventually devolve to something very

simple: Why is there a break from school during the last two weeks of December in Covington, Georgia? Answer: Christmas. Taking the logic further the question would be: Is there a consti-tutional prohibition from saying why the two-week break is taken (Christmas)? The answer would be, No, there is no consti-tutional barrier to calling Christmas what it is.

In Covington, Georgia, school board member Richard Tiede had no help from Christian legal groups, his own school board at-torney was advising against him, and Tiede had nowhere to turn.

Nationwide schools observe a Christmas holiday because the country is 84 percent Christian (using the Pew Poll Research Council's percentages for 2002); giving Christian students a Christmas break at Christmastime is simply an acknowledgment of the obvious: Experience tells school administrators that some-thing on the order of 84 percent of schoolchildren will simply not be in school on Christmas, nor on the days immediately be-fore and after. In fact, a Fox News poll from 2004 indicates that 96 percent of Americans celebrate Christmas. So it's a pretty safe assumption that all but 4 percent of the children of Covington would be home celebrating what they called Christmas during that break.

As a practical matter, what would be the point of staffing the classrooms with teachers, putting janitors on duty in the hall-ways, bringing the cafeteria workers in to make lunch, ordering the administrative staff to be at their desks if the students are not going to be on campus? The ACLU can call it an endorsement of religion, but school officials are going to shake their heads no, and say, We are just being realists.

No one is confused about these facts, yet for the ACLU, even acknowledging on the school calendar why school would be out of session for two weeks bracketing December 25 by printing the word "Christmas" in a little square on a calendar would be a crushing blow to the imaginary wall separating church and state, an outrageous and entirely impermissible violation of the Constitution of the United States, and totally forbidden, at least in Covington, Georgia, in the fall of 2000.

To the ACLU, it was nothing less than an intrusion of religion into the schools, a clear attempt by government (the school district) to establish an official religion, Christianity. It is Christians, after all, who observe December 25 as the day Jesus Christ was born, and it is Christians, after all, who call that day Christmas and the days around it the Christmas holidays.

Thinking back on it Goodmark warmed to the subject. "The practical problem with it is that children are people that live in Covington and Newton County and are entitled to go to these schools and not be coerced into participating in a Christmas holiday. They can take a break and it'll be a winter break and they'll participate in that. But to call it a Christmas holiday may not be applicable to them." Goodmark had his arguments all teed up and ready to go.

On the merits, Goodmark really had no case. His argument was all rhetoric and no case law. But one of the school board members, Richard Tiede, had inadvertently given the ACLU lawyer ammunition in the form of an ill-advised statement, and with that statement in hand Goodmark's feeble arguments didn't really matter. With the board member's statement made in public and on the record (and doubtless repeated a few times), the ACLU lawyer had the winning hand.

The issue had been bubbling for two years. One school board had scrubbed the word "Christmas" away, leading inevitably to a new school board that seemed to have realized what had been done and had tried to undo the damage.

As the leader of the Christmas restoration movement fifty-three-year-old Richard Tiede was a little out of his depth. His wife, Nancy, was a teacher in Covington High School, and he had decided to run for the school board out of a simple sense of contributing to the community. Tiede was an accounting instructor at the county technical college. He had retired from the Air Force as a captain in the satellites operation. According to his wife, Tiede liked to say he "flew" satellites from his position in the ground control operations center in Sunnyvale, California. He and Nancy had moved to Covington, Georgia, seeking a quiet place for quiet time. Tiede liked to ride his motorcycle for relaxation, a hobby which led to his death. In 2004 he was killed in a motorcycle accident, when he rounded a corner and was struck by a vehicle that was illegally and entirely unexpectedly driving backward.

But in the fall of 2000 Tiede decided the name on the school calendar designating the Christmas break ought to tell the truth. As far as he was concerned it was the Christmas break, and he thought the calendar should reflect that.

What Tiede said that gave Goodmark the victory before he even drove down from Atlanta was the following short, declarative statement: "America is a Christian nation."

It was a faux pas, and a fateful one at that.

That statement gave Goodmark the chance to argue against

the word "Christmas" and the likelihood to win in court when otherwise there was no legal basis for objecting and banning the word "Christmas."

Goodmark still argues the use of the word is wrong. "You can call it that, and you can call it that in your house. And I can call it that. And I can call it that on the street. But when the government calls it that, it becomes an endorsement of religion," Goodmark said confidently, while ignoring the national Christmas tree, which the president lights in an annual ceremony, the federal Christmas holiday, and other governmental acknowledgments of Christmas.

"That might be the case," he responded. "But this is a state and a state entity. And the standards would be different. I think that the point is more than the formalities of changing the word, it's the effect of it and the message that it sends."

Was Goodmark able to cite even one decision from the United States Supreme Court that would have the effect of forbidding the use of the word "Christmas" on a school calendar?

Goodmark immediately laughed, nervously. "Oh—no, I don't think there would be something as specific as that from the Supreme Court. And I don't even know if I still have my notes. But there's ample authority to say that the government can't establish a religion. I think that you would find ample authority for the general proposition that the government can't endorse one religion over the other. Do you not agree that calling something a Christmas holiday would be an endorsement of Christianity over the absence of religion?"

Well, no. Almost nobody agrees with that. Importantly, school board member Richard Tiede would not have agreed.

Richard Tiede may not have been able to express it well, but he knew Goodmark was wrong. "Rich felt that Christmas had become more than just a religious holiday," Nancy Tiede explained in an interview with the author. "He felt that it was a holiday that was recognized to one extent or another by people of different faiths, people of no faith."

Tiede said her husband thought Christmas "was something that was, in a way, uniquely American but had spread to other countries, and that Christmas had not necessarily been celebrated as much as it is now." Tiede thought Christmas had become materialistic and he would like to have seen the holiday return to traditions that were less so.

Nancy said she and her husband were not evangelical Christians, and not regular churchgoers, but that he held Christmas in special esteem because he thought Christmas had become a uniquely American holiday. To Tiede Christmas was a time for families to be together, a time for giving gifts to express affection and love, a time to sum up the year with close relations, and in his mind, a very secular American holiday. Far from being a religious zealot, Tiede was a classic American secularist: tolerant of all religions; appreciative of the people around him; willing to work for the good of his community; and committed to telling the truth, even if it was in small ways like calling the holiday what it was.

In proposing the change to his fellow board members Tiede might have said what his wife said he believed, that Christmas was a secular American holiday of a higher rank than, say, Super Bowl Sunday, but still secular. Instead he remarked that "America is a Christian nation" and that the school calendar should reflect the country's Christian roots. Those were the words that shall not be spoken.

For Tiede, renaming the break as Christmas simply reflected

reality, but the phrase "This is a Christian nation" constitutes one of the most dependable trip wires of our era.

Considering the highly charged atmosphere of the time, the board had originally summoned the courage to reject the advice of its own lawyer, who had counseled against the change back to the word "Christmas." But when Goodmark confronted them with Tiede's statement about America being a Christian nation, and their own lawyer admitted that that statement might give a judge an opportunity to find that the word change was not being done for a good enough reason, and he impressed upon them the fact that they would probably lose in court, they backed down.

This was, after all, a period when nativity scenes were being banned from schools outright, school prayer was a thing of the far distant past, and Christmas trees were undergoing a transformation from secular symbol to religious symbol, a change that was occurring entirely by executive fiat, by declarations of school boards and municipal officers in various communities all over the country.

Sam Harben, the lawyer who represented the Newton County school board in Covington, said in an Associated Press report, "If there were litigation"—and no one expected the ACLU would *not* sue—"the courts may well conclude there was not a valid, secular reason on the part of the board for a change."

Harben was no doubt thinking of Tiede's statement, on the record, that he wanted the change because "America is a Christian nation." If that were the reason for the change, Harben may well have been correct in concluding that the courts might have found that the board had not had a secular reason that would justify the change. After all, there had not been another, secular reason stated by the board. The primary reason ("This is a Christian nation") enunciated by Tiede certainly did not sound like a secular reason.

The ACLU had the school district, and its lawyer, and Rich Tiede over a barrel all because Tiede had described the reason for the change in such overtly Christian terms.

"We're a rural community here," Nancy Tiede said. "We have churches on every corner. We're close to Atlanta, but we don't have the property values that Atlanta does, and we're still just changing from being agricultural to exurban." The economics were weighing on Rich Tiede. "So, with No Child Left Behind and other mandates, the school systems are just reeling without any money. They're trying to do the best they can for the kids. And this seemed like something that was not worth pursuing if it meant having to spend money to do so."

Lawyer Sam Harben clearly might have consulted his fellow lawyers at the National School Boards Association in Washington, D.C., which might have tried to find solid constitutional ground for the position board member Tiede wanted to take. Harben took the ACLU's position, doubtless defensively, and concerned about the tidal wave of legal filings that would surely wash over him from the local offices of the ACLU.

It certainly made things simpler that Harben thought the board should stand down. For one thing, as one might expect, the ACLU lawyer agreed. Goodmark was reported by the newspaper to have said that if the board had made the change on the calendar quietly it probably would not have become an issue. (Years later Goodmark said, "I wouldn't have said something like that.") But since the issue was raised in a public meeting, and since board member Richard Tiede had said, on the record, that he wanted the change because "America is a Christian nation," then the courts would examine the record and in all probability conclude that the change was in fact an endorsement of a particular religion, Christianity, in violation of the establishment clause of the U.S. Constitution.

Faced with the consequence of his own words, Tiede reluctantly backed down. He could not, in good conscience, insist on an action that could incur legal costs his district could not afford, especially if his own lawyer was telling him the board would lose. He changed his vote, consigning the word "Christmas" to the "banned-in-Covington" list, but sputtered in frustration to a newspaper reporter that the ACLU was engaged in extortion and acting like the mob. Another board member, exasperated at the trap set and sprung by the ACLU lawyer, said the ACLU had practiced "bullying and intimidation."

It didn't matter to the school board or ACLU lawyers that board member Tiede was not an evangelical Christian intent on proselytizing his religion. It didn't matter that Tiede simply thought of Christmas as a uniquely American holiday that was essentially an observance of family, not religious, ties. What mattered was that Tiede had uttered words that recognize a reality all Americans know to be true, even those in a religious minority: America is an *overwhelmingly* Christian nation, founded by Christians who expressed their political beliefs in the context of their personal religiosity, and while the country was open and tolerant of other religions, its essential Christian character had not changed since the founding of the nation. In short, Tiede had been too honest, too accurate, too correct, too Christian.

The secularists, the humanists, the religionists other than Christian do not want to hear the reality that they are a very small minority of non-Christians in a sea of Christians that stretches to the horizons in all directions. Tiede had given voice to a sentence of reality that is forbidden to be spoken aloud.

Goodmark himself knew nothing of what Tiede really intended. He was surprised to learn five years later that Tiede wasn't a religionist at all, that he wasn't an evangelical Christian and had had no ties to Christian churches or groups trying to gain access to school campuses.

In fact, upon learning about Tiede, Goodmark sounded a little sorry for the school board member who had just said the wrong thing. "I'm sure that taking somebody out of context like that and then putting him in the public domain is a very difficult thing."

So Rich Tiede was convinced to vote against his own proposal. The word "Christmas" would not make a comeback in Covington, Georgia.

"I think he was disappointed," his wife said, a year after he died. "And, ironically, you know, we used to joke about it and say, Well, you know the worst thing that can happen is that they're gonna put on your tombstone: 'You believed in Christmas.'

"The bottom line is it just didn't make sense," Nancy Tiede said. "There are other school systems that have Christmas on their calendar. The University of Georgia's system had at that time holidays specified as Christmas holidays. It just seems ridiculous that this little-bitty school system couldn't call it what it really was. We couldn't call it Christmas."

What makes the tempest in Covington, Georgia, in the winter of 2000 more typical than not is the pattern. Citizen school board members, uneducated in the ways of the law, take a political stand, such as recognition of Christmas because "America is a Christian nation," as Tiede said. Often such statements are sim-

ply a political or rhetorical position devised and declared because
someone thinks it is right. Not necessarily smart, or wily, or
cagey, or wise . . . but right, correct, or accurate.

As in the case of Covington, Georgia, the ACLU objects, and in
an argument about the rightness or wrongness of calling a school
break by the name it has always been called (Christmas), those with
lesser skills in thinking like lawyers are outwitted by those whose
skills at lawyering are honed to a sharp and deadly edge. As the
ACLU lawyer pointed out, if the Covington, Georgia, school
board had just made the change with no announcement, no religious pronouncement, no amateur historical observation of the nation as a Christian country, then the ACLU would not have the
evidence that would convince a court that the change was under-
taken for a constitutionally impermissible reason. But since a
school board member had spoken up, since they had stated their
reasons as their beliefs that America is a Christian nation, the game
was effectively over. Check and checkmate.

By this method a collection of radical secularists, led by local
chapters of the ACLU and occasionally by the New York–based
parent organization, have invaded places where Christmas is held
in special affection (if not sacred) and have launched an attack on
every symbol of the day that has been traditionally observed as
the day of the birth of Jesus Christ. Christmas carols cannot be
sung, Christmas trees may not be displayed, and in at least one
case, even the colors red and green have been expunged in order
to make sure no notice is paid to the day 84 percent of the country believes is holy.

"The ACLU only asked the school board to comply with the

constitutional standards," Goodmark said in an Associated Press report. "The ACLU does not bully. The ACLU only asks that government bodies comply with the Constitution of the United States."

Mr. Goodmark misstates the case. The ACLU does bully, it does intimidate, and it demands local governmental bodies comply with ACLU directives, not with the Constitution of the United States, at least not the one interpreted by the Supreme Court of the United States. The ACLU demands local government go much further in expunging Christianity from schools and from municipal government locations than what is required by the Constitution and the U.S. Supreme Court, and the ACLU is well aware of what it is doing. For instance, the northern California ACLU advisory to parents and teachers on Christmas displays states clearly the Supreme Court has not banned certain Christmas displays such as Christmas trees, but advises against them anyway. In fact, the tactics and strategies of the ACLU in its war on Christmas are the very definition of bullying, and to avoid costly and time-consuming litigation from the ACLU, school boards and local governments frequently submit to ACLU demands that far exceed the limitations on religious observance on government property that is actually required by the law.

In the intervening years, of course, Richard Tiede has died and the town of Covington, Georgia, has moved on. But the question he raised by making a statement still deserves an answer. Is America a Christian nation?

If numbers count for anything at all, the answer is an emphatic yes.

It is worthwhile to briefly note the numbers game. The United States is overwhelmingly Christian. It is true that the percentage of self-identified Christians has dropped from decade to decade, but it is still an imposing majority, and no other religious group can compete in pure numbers. The Jewish population was 1.3 percent in 2002, and the Muslim population less than half that. Undoubtedly the Muslim population has grown since, but only the most dreamy and delirious statistician has projected the Muslim population to overtake or even challenge the Christian population.

What continues to erode the total percentage of Christians is the number of people who declare no religion at all, undoubtedly a high percentage of which were born Christian, into Christian families, but for reasons of secularism, or rejection of organized religion, or the siren call of atheism, or becoming signatories in spirit of the secular Humanist Manifesto III have decided they are not theistic enough to have committed to any particular religious discipline. The numbers say ten years ago 7 percent of those who identified themselves as Christian now say they have no religion.

Since the United States Census Bureau is forbidden by law from asking about religious identification, it refers those who want that information to private studies, and the census itself uses privately generated numbers for its own analysis. The most quoted, and perhaps the most authoritative since the 2000 census, is a study of the United States population in March 2001. It shows the percentage of Christians in the United States dropped from 86 percent in 1990 (that number derived from a sample of over two hundred thousand people) to 77 percent in 2000. The later survey sampled fifty-five thousand people, which is only a quarter the size of the 1990 survey, but is still an enormous sample by standards of election-year polling. This study was completed by the Graduate Center of the City University of New York, by Barry Kosmin, Egon Mayer, and Arieia Keysar and is titled, "The American Religious Identification Survey, 2001" (ARIS-2001).

By contrast the Pew Research Council study of two thousand people in 2002 showed Christians as 84 percent of the country.

As referred to earlier, the ARIS-2001 contained this fascinating note:

The greatest increase in absolute as well as percentage terms has been among those adults who do not subscribe to any religious identification; their number has more than doubled from 14.3 million in 1990 to 29.4 million in 2001; their proportion has grown from just about eight percent of the total in 1990 to over fourteen percent in 2001.

In 2001 some 27 million people said they followed no religion, another nine hundred thousand said they were atheists, who believe there simply is no god, and almost a million said they were agnostic, a doctrine which holds that the existence or nonexistence of God is unknown and unknowable.

So who is it saying the United States of America is not a Christian nation? Whoever makes such a statement has to be referring to something other than the facts before us, and of course they are: It is the constitutional stance of the nation to which they refer, the idea contained in the First Amendment to the Constitution that says: "Congress shall make no law respecting an establishment of religion, or prohibiting the free exercise thereof . . ."

The Fourteenth Amendment to the Constitution attaches local officials, even as lowly as a school board, to the prohibitions of that first amendment. And so it is always a question whether a government action in regard to religion tends to establish an official or favored religion, or does such government action tend to discourage or prohibit the free exercise of religion?

Did the late Richard Tiede give favor to Christianity with his statement or did he state a fact, which if taken into proper consideration by the school board and the courts might have made certain the school district was not exhibiting hostility or scorn or prohibition of a religion that celebrates a certain holiday known as Christmas?

In terms of his observational acumen, Tiede was certainly right. The United States is a Christian nation in terms of its population groups. Fallen or disaffected Christians in the latest survey make up a population six times as large as Jews and Muslims combined, and none of those population groups poses any sort of serious numerical challenge to Christians.

The numbers contained in these surveys tell another story as well: the story of the large number of self-identified Christians for whom Christmas is the one day of the year they make any sort of religious observation. What is the nature of that group? Are they easily persuaded to push the society ever more secular, to push out of the public eye the few remaining (and tenuous) symbols of a Christian holiday? Will they go along with the tiny minority of Jews, Muslims, atheists, agnostics, and religion-free secularists to suppress the religion of the supermajority?

These questions are history now in Covington, Georgia. Winter break is here to stay.

CHAPTER 2

MUSTANG, OKLAHOMA:

NATIVITY SCENE, BAD; KWANZAA AND HANUKAH, GOOD

Mustang, Oklahoma, is as red state as they come. A community of thirteen thousand, according to the 2000 U.S. Census, it has seventy-five hundred students in its school district. Mustang is a bedroom community of Oklahoma City, approximately fifteen miles to the northeast. It is 90 percent white, with very small ethnic and religious minorities. Twice as many Native Americans live in Mustang as Hispanics, and African Americans make up just over half of 1 percent of the population. Mustang is as white as white gets, and it is home to more than two dozen Christian churches and no mosques or synagogues.

It is one of the last places in America one would expect to find a dispute over Christianity—over Christmas—but that is exactly what happened in December 2004.

It had been a two-decade-long tradition in Mustang's Lakehoma Elementary school to put on a Christmas pageant for the Christmas season. Included in the pageant was a nativity scene, as well as references to Kwanzaa and Hanukah. To most parents in Mustang the Christmas pageant was as politically correct as it needed to be, and so they were shocked when the superintendent of schools, Karl Springer, suddenly issued an order days before the curtain was to rise on the school production that the nativity scene would be cut from the pageant, and a rumor circulated that the students would not be allowed to sing "Silent Night."

Shelly Marino, who had a third-grader in the school, spoke for hundreds, if not thousands, of other Mustang parents when she said, "How can this be? We live in the buckle of the Bible belt. This is Mustang, for goodness' sake."

Adding insult to injury, the Kwanzaa and Hanukah aspects of the Christmas pageant were to remain.

The news media picked up the story, and it was not only amplified throughout Oklahoma, but the wider world as well. The *Taipei Times* in Taiwan carried a story, as well as the BBC and other international news organizations. All the stories carried the same sense of shock that comes with every man-bites-dog story: How could this happen in Mustang, Oklahoma, of all places?

Superintendent Springer got over two thousand e-mails. The phone switchboard at the school district offices was flooded with protest calls. Springer was ridiculed and pilloried in the media nationwide, as talk radio picked up the story and spent days and days debating whether Karl Springer was Satan himself or just one of his misbegotten sons.

Springer, fiftyish and a father and grandfather, was a former U.S. Marine and a retired colonel in the Army Reserve. He had spent his entire career in education, rising from teacher to principal to superintendent. He was born in Hollywood, California, and spent the first three years of his life there. Even though he had not been back to his birthplace since shortly after he learned to walk, the angry media painted him as a Hollywood liberal who had come to Oklahoma schools only after leaving his best friend

Michael Moore back in Hollywood. It was all distortion and a tidal wave of vicious attacks on Springer. He took it like a Marine, silently enduring the abuse.

Nobody asked Springer why he had done it, or if they did, they hadn't listened to the answer. Springer had been advised by the school district's lawyer, whom he told me he had consulted after receiving complaints from some parents and the ACLU, that the nativity scene and perhaps even "Silent Night" could violate the establishment clause of the First Amendment to the U.S. Constitution. What if they were sued by an ACLU attorney, the same fear felt in Covington, Georgia? Springer said he felt he was honorbound to abide by his attorney's advice. To do otherwise might expose his school district to a lawsuit that it might lose, and to the attendant expenses of paying the court costs of the plaintiffs who might have brought the suit. Karl Springer felt he was in a box, and he had to make a difficult decision for the good of the Mustang School District.

Protesters surrounded the school district offices carrying signs that read NO CHRISTMAS, NO CHRIST, KNOW CHRISTMAS, KNOW CHRIST.

Neither the ACLU or any of its litigious cohorts had either filed suit or threatened a lawsuit. But they were in the back of Springer's mind. "It was the most difficult decision I've ever had to make," he said. "I had two strong legal opinions that something we had planned could be illegal. I wanted to make sure we protected our community from some kind of lawsuit."

Springer paused frequently as we spoke in our recorded interview a few months after the controversy. He was careful not to say anything that might reopen the wounds of the terrible fight of 2004.

Springer knew the attorney for the district had given him a legal opinion that was dynamite with a burning fuse. But he felt he had had no choice but to follow the advice. "You go to your attorney," Springer said in an interview with me. "And the attorney basically is going to give you the most conservative kind of decision that they can make. She basically gave us an opinion that . . . well, once we had that opinion, had we been sued over this the first thing that would happen would be the insurance carrier would come to the superintendent and say, 'Well, tell me, sir, what did your attorney have to say about this?' And if you say, Well, I talked to one, and I'm certainly not going to perjure myself, I'm always going to tell the truth, but once you do that, then the protection of the insurance company with the school district is going to be gone."

Recalling the bind he was in still gives Springer the willies. "Probably if I hadn't talked to an attorney, it would have been more of a 50/50 kind of a thing. But once you talk to an attorney, and they tell you that this particular thing could be problematic for you and could be illegal, then you must act. You must act in good faith to what you've been advised."

Karl Springer had been advised that even though his community was, in all probability, over 90 percent Christian, and there probably was not a Jewish person, or a Hindu, or a Muslim, or even an atheist anywhere near Mustang who would bring a suit, if there were, and they did, he would lose. Out of fear of a lawsuit that would probably not materialize, Karl Springer felt he had to do the prudent thing and ban the nativity scene, though he claims he didn't order "Silent Night" to be silent.

Of course, lawsuits may not have been the worst possibility for Springer. What he really had to fear, immediately, were voters.

Two weeks after the pageant decision voters went to the polls and defeated an $11 million bond issue for a new elementary school and a new fleet of school buses. The protest vote was not huge, but it was decisive: The no votes deprived the Mustang School District of the 60 percent yes vote required for passage. No Christmas, no bonds.

It was a stinging, humiliating defeat, and Springer had no one to blame but himself. The bond issue failed by only five percentage points, meaning that well more than half the community voted for it, but no one was confused about why that 5 or 6 percent of the voters came out to vote against improved school facilities for their own children. It was a rebuke to Karl Springer and the attorney for the district and the board of education—and anybody else who had anything to do with the decision.

In the smoldering ashes of defeat Karl Springer realized he had a long-term problem, and he began to search for a way out of this grave crisis in Mustang.

"I remembered that there was problem in Tulsa a while back," he said, describing a flash of memory at the depths of his despair. "So I contacted the school superintendent up there." The school superintendent in Tulsa gave Springer a name and a phone number and Springer called. He found himself talking to Dr. Charles Haynes of the First Amendment Center in Washington, D.C.

The First Amendment Center was founded in 1991 by longtime journalist and newspaper editor John Seigenthaler, who retired from the Nashville *Tennessean* after a forty-three-year career as a reporter, editor, publisher, and CEO of the newspaper. Seigenthaler also took a break from newspapering to work for Robert F. Kennedy's Justice Department during the civil rights struggle, and was once attacked by a mob of Klansmen. His son,

John Seigenthaler, Jr., is an anchor for NBC News and one of the founding anchors at MSNBC, where he was—and remains—a friend and colleague of this author.

Dr. Haynes is a senior scholar at the center and author of the influential book *Finding Common Ground: A Guide to Religious Liberty in the Public Schools*. He has spent years working on the problem of what seemed to him to be a growing intolerance for religion, particularly Christianity, in public schools, and he had been instrumental in finding solutions in several school districts around the country where the conflict had reached a point of crisis.

"Dr. Haynes, obviously, was very knowledgeable about what our issue was to me. And, it was kind of a strange conversation," Springer said to me. It was strange because Haynes knew exactly what Springer's problem was. He had dealt with it many times before, and had in fact made something of a career out of rushing in as if he were driving an ambulance, lights flashing and sirens blaring, after schools had made disastrous policy decisions on restricting religious liberty in schools. "Dr. Haynes was so very encouraging. And he understood that we were trying to do the right thing. And that we just needed to work together as a community to develop some policy so that we would be able to have a maximum kind of religious liberty in our school system."

Karl Springer was keenly aware that his was a religious community. He just didn't know how to go about integrating that reality into the schools. The specter of the ACLU or one of its cohort secularist groups, always ready with a lawyer, a letter, and demands, hung over his shoulder.

Haynes had a great deal of sympathy for Springer and the Mustang school district. Although he didn't think Springer had done the right thing, he also understood why Springer had taken the action that he had. He had seen it many times before, and he had often seen someone like Karl Springer good-heartedly committing the sin of bad decisions that come from good intentions. "I think he's just one of these people who sort of believes you ought to do what's right whether it's popular or not," Haynes said of Springer. "And he knew that it wouldn't be a popular decision. I mean, he was aware of the potential for people to be upset. He's been there a while. He's well respected in the community and as the superintendent. So, I think he just felt, 'This is my call at this point. I'm gonna do it.'"

What was wrong with Springer's decision?

"If there was a mistake made there, it was the way the decision was made," Haynes said. "And I think that any time a decision about what to do at Christmas is made just before Christmas, the school district is setting itself up for an ugly fight. It's the worst time to address the issue, even if you think something illegal or unconstitutional might be going on. My advice always is to wait until January or February before you sit down and sort of revisit your policy."

Haynes's primary rule is, "First, do no harm."

"It's just terrible when people had practiced something or planned something that they've done for years and then just suddenly say, 'We're not gonna do it this year,' right before the event. So, I think that was really the problem."

It was part of the problem. The overarching issue was the same one that confronts public schools all over the country: Does religion have to be banned from public schools? Haynes said no.

He and his colleagues had been working on this precise question for two decades. "We decided to tackle this religious holidays issue because it's a perennial fight. We jokingly called it the 'December dilemma' back then," Haynes said. A former divinity student, not a lawyer, Haynes was determined to sort out denominational or faith differences in order for religion to have a place in the public schools.

"We brought together groups and said, 'You know, can we do something just on religious holidays?' And some of the groups at the time said, 'Don't even call a meeting. You know we've been fighting about this a long time. And we're just at a standoff, and either we have people who want the nativity pageant and so forth, or we have people who don't want anything at all, but we're just not going to find common ground.'"

Haynes paused. "But we did."

In the early 1990s Haynes spent four months negotiating with hotly contentious religious groups to come up with model national guidelines on religion in schools that all the groups at the table could sign on to.

"The National Association of Evangelicals, Christian Legal Society, American Jewish Congress, teachers unions, school boards . . . a pretty good variety. Not everybody in the world, but that was the beginning of crafting what I call the third approach, that's neither the sacred public school of our early history nor the more recent phenomena of this *naked* public school, where all religion is kept out."

Out of this experience Haynes's group had devised an approach that could be used in a place like Mustang, Oklahoma, where the feelings were raw, the hurt was obvious to anybody, and the fear of being sued colored every decision.

"The whole reason I started these national guidelines in the first place was to help that local community have some kind of safe harbor," Haynes said, "so that the national groups, or at least some of them, on both sides, could say to the local school districts, 'If you do this, it will work, and we won't sue you. We'll support you.'"

Springer was looking for a way out of his dilemma and Haynes seemed to be it. He invited Haynes to fly from Washington, D.C., to Mustang and meet with a group of community leaders, religious and secular, to see what could be worked out.

"I think that the basic thing that I personally wanted was exactly what the community wanted. And that was to be able to teach about religion, to be able to find some strategies and some ways of being able to discuss religion in our schools," Springer said in an interview with me. "To be able to talk about religion. To be able to educate about religion. And to be able to do that in a way that didn't seek to promote one religion over another religion. The issue was striving for awareness of different religions and the historical impact that they had had on world history, United States history."

There was no policy on religion at the Mustang schools, except a couple of sentences in the policy guide on time off for religious holidays. So, for Springer the goal was, in his words, "to develop a policy that focused on teaching about religion, not *practicing* religion in school."

Springer was still licking his wounds from the enormous firestorm of protest over his original cancellation of the Christmas pageant nativity scene, the incorrect but damaging report of the silencing of "Silent Night," and the subsequent defeat of a very important school bond issue. But he saw there was no way out except to go forward to a place where he would not again be put in the position of having to accept legal advice that would cause so much trouble in his community. "I thought that we would be able to open all sorts of doors all over the United States that are closed to school districts because, you know, the concept of teaching about religion is one that hasn't been embraced everywhere. And, it requires quite a bit of work."

As Springer embarked on this project it appeared that the attitude in many school districts in the United States was that the way to stay neutral on a religious question was simply to not deal with it at all. The campaign by the ACLU and People for the American Way and Americans United for the Separation of Church and State had worked all too well. Most school administrators have come to believe that religion could not be allowed on school grounds.

"I think that that's been the path of least resistance for lots of school districts, and one that's totally understandable when you add to that the fact that most school districts don't have a board policy on religion," Springer says in an interview today, months after the bitter experience of 2004. "So it's pretty difficult to approach education about religion in your school system if you don't have a policy that you know has been looked at and discussed and spent time over."

Springer resolved to do just that, to develop a bulletproof policy that would both stand up to a legal challenge and, in his words, "develop the structure and the organization for teaching about religion." He wanted a policy that any judge would approve that would develop "the issues that we will bring in to the curriculum. The curriculum issues, the things that we're going to be able to teach about religion, [would be] spelled out in our policy."

What Haynes and the First Amendment Center were able to show Springer was that the United States Supreme Court does allow religion to be discussed, it does allow Christmas carols to be sung, it does allow the word "Christmas" to be used; it would allow the use of a Christmas tree, a nativity scene, and the colors red and green. All of that would be allowed—and would be legal—if the context of the use in school were education.

"The approach that we're going to take to religion is important. Our approach is going to be academic and not devotional, basically trying to expose our students to religion in a way that does not seek to promote any faith or reject people who have no faith," Haynes said in one of several interviews with me. Charles Haynes has been long convinced that the First Amendment to the United States Constitution means exactly what it says: "Congress shall make no law respecting an establishment of religion; or prohibiting the free exercise thereof." For those who talk about an establishment clause and those who talk about the free exercise clause there should be no conflict. "What is constitutional is that public schools," said Haynes, "may certainly teach about the meaning of Christmas and should. They should let kids know what Christians believe about Christmas. They should have some historical context."

Haynes said he believes that this struggle over religion in the public schools has been going on since the inception of public schools in America. (In 1907 Jewish students in New York City staged a walkout and boycott of the public schools in protest of the overtly Protestant Christian curriculum and practices of the school system.) "I think what's going on is that we never got this right in our history and so we're struggling now to figure out just what it means to actually apply the First Amendment in a public school setting. In that struggle, we have people who are in public schools who are taking the schools in a direction that sometimes excludes religion, unconstitutionally or unfairly. We still have some people on the other end of the spectrum who still would like a particular religion to be favored and promoted through public schools. And so we have these two poles and we have most folks somewhere in the middle trying to figure out what the best approach is."

How is religion taught as history, for instance, without it being taught as a *belief*? Haynes said students "should know that not all Christians, for example, celebrate the birth of Jesus Christ in December; Orthodox celebrate it at a different time. They should know how Christians understand that sacred event."

What about the courts? "If we look at the the Supreme Court's various holiday display decisions over the years, and some of the things the Court has said, if not ruled, most of the justices have indicated that such things as a Christmas tree and those kinds of things are, for constitutional purposes, more secular symbols."

The Christmas tree, in other words, gets a green light, not a red light, from the courts, though Haynes said he thinks schools should still regard it with a yellow light of caution. "So it may be, in other words, constitutional to put up trees in classrooms in a public school, and to put greenery and mistletoe around the school and have Santa Claus visit the school. Any of what I call 'shopping mall Christmas' things may be constitutional, but for some non-Christians, those things still look like Christianity. And actually, for some practicing Christians, those things don't appear to them as Christmas at all, not in the religious sense. So in a way, the secular Christmas trappings trigger a fight and really don't make anybody happy in the end, after all the school does.

"If a school tries to accommodate religious Christians by saying, 'Well, we'll have the tree, and then we'll make other people happy by putting a menorah next to it in the hallway, and maybe we'll put Kwanzaa up,' all that does is trigger a fight from traditionalist Christians, who say, 'Well, we're not the tree, that doesn't represent Christianity. If you have a menorah, you've got to have the crèche.' And then the Jewish community and others say, 'Well, we didn't sign up for *that*. I mean, we can live with the tree as long as there's a menorah, but we don't want the crèche in there. That's too religious.'

"So, the school's trying to satisfy people by putting the shopping mall Christmas stuff around the school is probably a losing proposition. There's no constitutional barrier to doing it, but it's going to trigger fights and conflicts. And it's not the best way to go about handling Christmas."

The approach Haynes said he recommends is to forget the decorations and strive to educate. "And this model, I think, is a First Amendment public school, or a civil public school, I sometimes call it, where religion is treated with fairness and respect, but we make sure that school officials aren't in the business of either promoting or denigrating religion. Their job under the First Amendment is to be fair, neutral, honest brokers for everybody, to protect the rights of everyone, but not to take sides on religion."

But what about the symbols? Is it good enough to say to parents, "Your child will learn what Christians believe, what Jews believe, what Muslims believe, what Hindus believe, but at Christmastime you will still not have the Christmas tree in school"?

"For some Christians removing the tree is the last vestige of who they are in their schools. And, you know, Protestants didn't found public schools in the first place in order for them to turn into something completely secular. They just assumed that their values and who they are as people and their culture would still be the tone and spirit of the school and the curriculum."

Protestants may have watched their assumptions proven wrong. "As that has died away, in the twentieth century particularly, and the last remnants of their schools were sort of taken away, with the prayer decisions and the Bible reading decisions of the sixties, the frustration has just grown in that community. The schools no longer represent the kinds of values or even mention who they are.

"Some of them say things like, 'Well, you can have witches at Halloween but you can't mention Jesus in December.' And they think there's something deeply wrong with that. So on one side you have people who think, 'Well, unless we fight for this tree, I mean, as silly as it may sound, we have nothing left. I see you taking away the last thing or the last few things we have so that we can still say these are schools that we feel represent who we are.'"

Haynes is a soft-spoken man, which undoubtedly helps as he tries to negotiate these tricky issues. "On the other side, of course, you have people, non-Christians and liberal Christians and others who felt, 'We fought a long time to kind of get rid of the Protestant agenda in schools. We fought to remove the government from imposing a particular version of the Bible. There were Bible wars, for goodness' sakes, in the nineteenth century over whose Bible would be read in the public schools. So there was a long fight over what kind of culture we have in the schools and how we shape our nation,' So those people feel they've won by removing these state-sponsored religious practices and those symbols. And they see even secular Christmas symbols as kind of a throwback to that day, and a reminder of the time when a certain Protestant agenda ruled the schools. So, they see these symbolic fights as kind of an echo of those fights, and they don't want to lose any turf.

"That's one of the reasons it's so hard to get beyond these failed models, because people still carry around an attitude that it's winner take all. It's either schools as a religion-free zone or schools as my religion echoed in the practices and the symbols.

"I think they're both wrong, and neither [is] going to win the battle in the long term, because public schools won't survive under either of those models, in my view. So, there's got to be a new way."

In Mustang, Oklahoma, various religious groups, including the Protestant Christian evangelicals who are the supermajority of the local population, have accepted the Haynes model: education, not celebration.

It's been a godsend for Karl Springer.

He was almost giddy with excitement about the next step: preparing teachers for the new way to approach the question of religion in the schools.

"The teacher training and curriculum was an area where we felt that we needed to have some help," said Springer. Charles Haynes and his staff would return to Mustang to help prepare teachers for the new school year. "Dr. Haynes will talk to our elementary teachers and secondary teachers about the issues, about the policy that we've developed, and about some strategies that we can use to be able to embellish or enrich our curriculum with some education about religion. And I think what that does for us is that it makes it so that the issue of religion won't be one that is just in December, but it would be throughout the school year.

"A lot of the issues that we have right now with the educated people of our country have to do with a lack of knowledge about religion, the different religions in the world. And this is going to be a very positive thing for our students, and I think for our community, to be able to do it in a way where we have an educational goal."

Springer still gets the shivers thinking about the decision he faced without a policy that had been well thought out, that had been vetted by lawyers, that had the agreement of the religious leaders of the community. "When you are in a situation where something comes up and you don't have a policy, you wind up going for a legal opinion. And the legal opinion that you're going to have is going to be . . . it's going to be confining.

"A well-educated student, a well-educated citizen needs some information about religion. So from a school system standpoint, we plan on looking at including some of the major religions in our curriculum."

So looking back, what does Springer think now about Mustang's religious war? "You know, you talk about the way it affects you personally. I wasn't curled up in the corner in a fetal position or anything like that. I truly wanted to do the right thing."

For now, at least, the community is satisfied with the Mustang schools' new goal of making certain religion is in the classroom as a matter of history or literature or art, that students learn what different religions believe with the full understanding that no student is required to take on those beliefs him- or herself.

CHAPTER 3

BALDWIN CITY, KANSAS:

SANTA GETS BOUNCED BECAUSE IT'S DISCOVERED HE'S CHRISTIAN

What does Santa have to do to get fired? If he doesn't smell like whiskey on the job, if he's not a child molester trying to get close to kids, if he's not already wanted for other crimes, what does Santa have to do to get banned?

In Baldwin City, Kansas, Santa was bounced because he was a Christian, and the man who hired him was a Christian, and Santa was accused of making Christianity part of his act as the jolly old elf.

The Santa fight happened in December 2003, and when the Kansas dust had settled Santa Claus was, indeed, banned from the Baldwin City schools.

The questions were: Did Santa, while visiting schoolrooms of children in kindergarten and first and second grades, say something casual and essentially inoffensive about Jesus Christ, or did he enter the classrooms to spread the word of Jesus by stealth, in the guise of the friendly and jolly Christmas elf? Or was Santa being used as a scapegoat, a way to have revenge on a conservative Christian school superintendent by a small group of liberal activists over a related issue, Christianity itself?

When the questions were decided, Santa was fired, the conservative Christian school superintendent was still running the schools, the activist who had led the fight had moved out of town to friendlier territory in Lawrence, home of the University of Kansas, and the small Midwestern town was all but at arms.

Baldwin City is southwest of Kansas City, a bedroom suburb of Lawrence, Kansas, directly south. Unlike many suburbs and exurbs that were built from blank land, Baldwin City has a long history. Its people were pioneers who settled halfway across the continent, on the route west. Baldwin City is on the Santa Fe Trail, the main emigrant trail, in the years of its heavy use nothing more than a track running west. The trail was always intensely traveled but never either built or maintained, and it hardly qualifies as what we think of today as a road. Visitors may drive north to the outskirts of town to see a preserved section of prairie that still shows the deep ruts of the thousands of heavy wagons that passed through Baldwin City headed to California and Oregon.

Another tourist attraction around Baldwin City is a close neighbor, Black Jack, Kansas, the location of the first battle between proslavery and antislavery forces before the Civil War. Today visitors may also drive north to see the parts of the trail used by Quantrill's Raiders on their ride to fame for their murderous raid on Lawrence, Kansas.

Lawrence might be the only city in the nation founded for purely political reasons. In 1854 men and women from the New England Emigrant Aid Society founded Lawrence in an effort to keep the territory free of slavery. As a magnet for abolitionists and free-staters, Lawrence was under constant attack by proslavery forces. On August 21, 1863, Quantrill's Raiders killed two hundred men and boys in Lawrence in the worst atrocity of the Civil War.

Just to the south, Baldwin City in the mid 1850s stood at the crossroads of the temperance movement as it sought to ban "demon rum," and the Free-Soilers movement, which sought to ban the abomination of slavery. It was the spot where consumers and purveyors of alcohol and owners of slaves collided with determined reformers not easily dissuaded from their basic Christian way of life, their rock-ribbed personal morality, public duty, and religious beliefs.

Baldwin City is also the home of Baker University, the oldest university in Kansas, founded 147 years ago by what is now the United Methodist Church. The founder of methodism, John Wesley, cautioned against intolerance among members of various religions.

But both Baldwin City and Lawrence are in Douglas County, which is the only county out of 105 in the state of Kansas to vote for John Kerry in the 2004 presidential election. One hundred and four others voted for Bush, and were classified as thoroughly red.

Douglas alone in all of Kansas was completely blue. And one of the principals in the battle of Santa Claus, December 2003, remains certain to this day that Santa Claus was nothing more than a symbol of the differences between conservatives and liberals, between blue states and red states in the one county in the state where liberals were in control and the conservatives, mostly evangelical Christians, were the embattled minority.

In early December 2003 the Baldwin City school board fired Santa Claus, and the issue was clearly Christianity. The debate over Santa came in a meeting of the board of the Baldwin City schools, where Santa stood accused of proselytizing his personal religious views and those of the superintendent of schools, both of whom were members of the same Christian church, what is now known as the Grace Community Church. In fact, the man who played Santa was the assistant pastor of that church.

"This was not a case of Santa roaming down a hallway with a 'ho, ho, ho' while casually handing out candy canes," reported Stacy Cohen, who was on the school board, and who had a daughter in kindergarten at a school in the district. Stacy Cohen's young daughter told her "that she had gone to the gym for an assembly and Santa talked to them. The line that stuck with me was, 'If you believe in Jesus, Santa will bring you toys.'"

While that line certainly does sound coercive of a kindergartener, and while Cohen sticks by her child's recollection of events, the Baldwin City *Signal* reported no such coercion in its account of the story, and both the superintendent of schools and the man who played Santa Claus deny it vehemently.

In the published version the story began with a letter from the ACLU. In fall 2003 the Kansas branch of the American Civil Liberties Union complained to the Baldwin City school board of a "Sneaky Santa" as ACLU attorney Dick Kurtenbach put it. Santa's offense was an abuse of his privilege to visit children in the schools. The ACLU said Santa used his access to kids to proselytize one religion in particular, Christianity: "Christian clergy dressed in a Santa Claus suit may proselytize a sectarian message in USD 348 public schools in near future."

Directly contradicting board member Stacy Cohen's version of Santa's offense, the Baldwin City *Signal* newspaper reported that, according to the school superintendent, after the usual and expected round of ho-hos and dispensing of candy and a pencil, Santa would ask the children if they knew why Christmas was celebrated. When one or two youngsters would tentatively offer that Christmas was connected to the birth of Jesus (often the children were not absolutely certain), Santa "concurred."

The newspaper also reported that Superintendent James White responded to the ACLU and Cohen at the school board meeting. He said that Santa had been visiting the schools to distribute candy canes to students for the previous several years. He reminded the board that the district even owned two Santa suits so that two Santas could efficiently make the rounds of district campuses. He had to admit that, yes, it was true that the previous year the assistant minister from his church had played the role of Santa Claus, mainly because the minister was fortunate enough to look so much like the real Santa. "You couldn't have a better Santa Claus," White said.

The board, Cohen included, wanted an exact description of Santa's actions. At each elementary school, White said, Santa asked the students why Christmas is celebrated. "In every school, one or more children would pop up and say, 'Jesus' birthday,'" he said.

White assured the board that even though Santa was an assistant minister, there was no way the students or teachers would know because Santa did not discuss religion further, but instead talked to the students about respecting parents and teachers as well as not smoking, drinking, or using drugs. According to the superintendent, the Santas were not proselytizing religion but urging clean living and civilized, respectful behavior on the part of the children.

"If that, in any way, can be proselytizing anyone, I certainly do apologize," White said. Two years later, Superintendent White remembered the details as if they were only yesterday. "Greg Childress plays the part of Santa Claus for many different organizations," White said in an interview. "I asked Greg if he had some time available on the given date to go around to our elementary buildings and share with the kids a little Christmas joy. And he said, 'Sure, I'd be glad to.'"

Childress was sixty-three years old, a little on the portly side, and wore his white beard long, Santa style. He had played Santa Claus in and around Baldwin City for various organizations for years. "The critical element there for me was the likeness of Greg to Santa Claus," White said, looking back. "It's just incredible. He's short, stubby, long white beard. White hair. And you didn't need to have a fake beard for Greg. He had it all."

Childress had been doing the Santa job for so long he had a routine. He told me in a recorded interview, "To most kindergarten, first, second, third graders, Santa Claus could be classified as a hero.

"So I usually try to talk to the kids a little bit about making good decisions, bad decisions. I usually tell them that—you know as they get a little older they're gonna make a lot more decisions than they're making now in their lives. And—and that if they make bad decisions there are sometimes consequences that have to be paid. And then I usually talk a little more about drugs, alcohol, tobacco, abstaining from those things.

"Then I usually always will say, 'Who can tell me why we celebrate Christmas?' And somebody will say, 'It's Jesus' birthday.' And so I'll say, 'That's exactly right. It's traditionally been the reason we celebrated Christmas is that it is Jesus' birthday.' And I said, 'You know if we didn't celebrate Jesus' birthday, you all and your teacher would probably be in school the next two weeks instead of getting ready to go out on holiday.'"

Whether he was in a classroom speaking to a small group of kids or in an auditorium speaking to an assembly, when he played Santa, Childress was always accompanied by Superintendent White, a point White emphasized in his interview with me.

"The possibilities that existed there were fantastic," Superintendent White said. "The kids would see someone that certainly was not dressed in a uniform. They'd see someone with a real beard and white hair and a ho, ho, ho.

"So then he goes around to the elementary buildings and he simply asked the kids if they knew why we celebrate Christmas. And, at every elementary school, at least one, and oftentimes quite a number more, would pop up and say, 'Because it's Jesus' birthday.' And then he would go on from that."

Superintendent White said Childress would "take that cue and say something to the effect that, Yes, that's the reason we celebrate. It's Jesus' birthday, and then he'd make a couple of other comments about them being good kids. And that certainly Santa would come to see them. And that they should be good to one another and good to their parents, and that was pretty much the size of each stop."

Did Childress ever say, "If you believe in Jesus, Santa will bring you toys"? This is precisely what Stacy Cohen said in an e-mail to me, that her daughter reported hearing.

Both White and Childress deny this. "I was present at every one of his presentations," said White. "He never said anything of the sort."

"I would never say anything like that," said Childress.

Both sides insist the other's version of events is not correct.

So who reported Santa? White doesn't know, because when the ACLU came into the case the identity of the complainant was not revealed. "At one of the stops, a parent took exception to him asking the students if they knew why we celebrated Christmas. They didn't like the idea of the kids stating the fact that we celebrate Christmas to celebrate Jesus' birthday," White said, who added he did not know the identity of anyone who complained.

Even though White and Childress are practicing Christians and attend the same church, both said they did not think it would be right for Santa Claus to say anything more to kids about the reason for Christmas than simply to acknowledge it was the day the birthday of Jesus was celebrated.

"They were trying to say that by asking that question, as a Christian minister, he was trying to proselytize kids into his faith," White said, looking back.

So the Western Missouri Chapter of the American Civil Liberties Union came to Baldwin City with the threat of a lawsuit if Santa were allowed to visit school classrooms again. "I think that there are those that feel like it is an entanglement of church and state whenever you mention the name of Jesus. And whether it's answering a question or whether it's a true statement, that has no bearing," White said.

The superintendent never did face the accuser, because whoever it was who reported the Santa allegation to the ACLU never made him- or herself public.

"If they could get the ACLU to take up their cause, and [they could] remain anonymous, which is exactly what happened, then they wouldn't have to withstand any scrutiny from other parents in the community," White said. "And that's the reason that they didn't come to the board. Whether it was 'they,' I don't know. It may have only been one person. But, I'm going to say 'they' because I assume there was more than one person involved."

Whether it was one or two or more, it wasn't many. What was clear from my e-mail exchange with her was that the ACLU and the complaining party had an ally on the school board: Stacy Cohen. "I know extremists say there shouldn't be anything about Christmas in the public schools. I disagree with that, as have the courts," Cohen said, writing of the incident almost two years later. "We are still a predominately Christian nation, and Christmas is our biggest holiday. However, no student should be forced to question his own religion or be confused at school by Christian teachings."

Superintendent White and board member Cohen were at odds at the time, and they are at odds now. "I just don't see how the question that was asked could be construed to mean anything other thing it was Jesus' birthday," White said. As far as White is concerned it would be no different than telling students on a certain day that it was Buddah's birthday or the prophet Muhammad's birthday.

But Cohen remained adamant. "While there are not that many Jewish students in Baldwin," she continued in a written response to the author's questions, "there are a number of fundamentalist Christian families who celebrate Jesus' birth but not the commercialism of the holiday, which includes Santa. It is confusing for them because they love Jesus and believe in him, but Santa doesn't visit them.

"My last name is Cohen—a very Jewish name—but I am not Jewish, nor is my husband," Stacy Cohen said. "We celebrate Christmas and all other Christian holidays. I realized after working around Jewish kids that Santa is secular for people who lean toward Christianity, but who aren't very religious, but for everyone else—Jews, Muslims, etc.—Santa is not a part of their world—ever."

The ACLU of Kansas agreed with Cohen. Santa had gone too far. Santa had trampled the Constitution. The ACLU attorney called Greg Childress "Sneaky Santa," the most quotable phrase of the incident.

"He was sneaky. He took advantage of his access to children to preach, and that simply cannot be allowed to happen," said Dick Kurtenbach of the Western Missouri ACLU, which made the complaint that wound up before the Baldwin City school board.

The board and its superintendent seemed shocked and contrite. Had Greg Childress, everybody's favorite Santa, suddenly turned rogue? "We need to make sure we're doing the right thing for all our kids," board president Ed Schulte said. "We need to make sure we're not promoting one religion over another religion."

"I see it as a message of education," the superintendent pleaded at the board meeting. "If we try to hide the fact [that] it's Jesus' birthday, I think that's inaccurate. That's the reason we celebrate it."

On the night of the school board meeting Stacy Cohen didn't like the superintendent's explanation and plainly didn't buy it. She was quoted in newspaper reports saying that parents should have been notified of Santa's visit and should have been given a chance for their children to opt out of the exposure to Santa Claus. Cohen also told the board she was bothered by how much attention Christmas got in school activities during this time of year. The newspaper account reported that Cohen had used her daughter's class project—a paper chain that counted down the days to Santa's visit on Christmas—as an example of a school activity that could possibly exclude some students. "A child that doesn't celebrate Santa, what are they counting down to?" she was quoted as saying.

That made no sense to the superintendent. "With all the Christmas pageantry and hoopla that takes place from the first of December until December twenty-sixth to the thirtieth, whenever people quit taking gifts back to exchange them," White said in an interview looking back on events, "I don't know that anyone that has attended any school, whether public or private, doesn't have an understanding of what's taking place."

It was clear that Santa was being fired because Santa and the man who hired him were Christian and some people wanted Christianity barred at the schoolhouse door.

"My daughter brought home something Christmas related nearly every day during the month of December. How would I have felt if we were Jewish?" Cohen wrote, summarizing her Christmas from hell. "The 4th, 5th and 6th grade musical in December is usually Christmas connected. One of our new professors at Baker University in 2003, who was Jewish, had his daughter in 6th grade that year. How did she feel about having to practice Christmas songs every day for weeks on end? Most schools do a mix of songs, including non-Christmas ones, to be fair to all children."

White said that that is precisely what his schools did. "We do have Christmas programs. But we are very cognizant about including secular music in those Christmas programs as well. That's the reason we call them 'holiday' programs. No longer do we call them 'Christmas' programs."

Superintendent White's schools did not put up Christmas trees, either. However, that rule came into effect because of the fire marshal, not the Christmas police. "We don't put up any live trees anymore" said White, because of the fire danger. And since the schools couldn't put up a real tree, White thought it made no real sense to go and buy plastic trees. So Baldwin City schools had been treeless for a few years.

Superintendent Jim White is fifty-seven years old. He's lived in Kansas his whole life, and has spent thirty years in the schools as a teacher, principal, and now superintendent. But he is also an active member of a Christian church, and his opponents in the Santa case were clearly aiming at his Christian values.

For one thing, it had happened before, just a few months earlier. The same year as the great Santa debate at the school board meeting, before the Santa issue came up, Cohen and others had objected to a rule White had imposed on a certain teacher.

"Just prior to this incident, as a matter of fact in late August of the beginning of this school year," White says, "I had asked a teacher not to read a book out loud in class to students. And that became a tremendous issue in the district."

The book was *We All Fall Down* by Robert Cormier, which *Publishers Weekly* described this way: "an unapologetically severe story about four boys who victimize Karen Jerome and her family, Cormier once again explores the potential for malice in all of us. The teenagers leave the Jeromes' home in ruin; Karen is assaulted and subsequently hospitalized in a coma."

"The issue with the book was the language," said White, "coupled with a scene with three boys holding a girl up against a wall and gang-raping her. They were reading that out loud in class. And I told the teacher I didn't want it read out loud in class."

The out-loud reading had been done for the previous three years in a freshman orientation class taught by teacher Joyce Tallman. A complaint about the book had been lodged the previous spring but had slipped through the cracks of the bureaucracy. Now it was the start of school, and another teacher, who had a fourteen-year-old child in the orientation class, objected to the reading of the Cormier book.

The teacher brought the issue to the school board, and it became a cause célèbre in Baldwin City. "Some of these same people, and Stacy Cohen was very much involved in that, took me apart over that. They thought I was censoring the teachers."

White hadn't banned the book; he hadn't had it removed from the library; he hadn't told the teacher the book could not be assigned to be read for class; he had simply said he didn't want it read out loud in class. "That caused a firestorm. And that occurred just before this Christmas thing. And I will never be convinced that this Christmas thing didn't come up as a result of that book issue."

Superintendent White couldn't understand why passages about gang rape were to be read out loud to fourteen-year-old high school freshmen. "Are you trying to convince kids that it's a part of life? That some girls are just going to get raped? I, I, I don't know," he stammered. "I just can't imagine the numbers of people that got up in the open meetings and said, 'We shouldn't censor that. If that's what the teacher thinks is important to read, then we shouldn't censor it.'"

White compounded the problem by making a personal comment that led his critics to charge he was trying to impose his conservative Christian values on the kids he was hired to educate.

"I was picked apart because one of my comments was, 'I

wouldn't want my granddaughter to have to sit in class and listen to that.' And I was ripped in the paper and on-line."

White is absolutely convinced he took the right position. "I've just never been able to understand how anybody found that acceptable. That they would want their kids read that out loud in the classroom. I didn't then, I don't now, and I don't know that I ever will."

The issue of White's personal views was never far from the surface. "I think some people felt like I did this just because of my values. And that I shouldn't have compared what I would have done for my granddaughter with what's taking place in school."

Stacy Cohen was livid. "The book was pulled without the board reviewing it based on one or two parents complaining," she said. "I don't get that at all."

The controversy raged on for three months. In October Cohen was still angry that action was taken on the basis of a small number of complaints. "One or two parents should not be allowed to dictate what the rest of the school can read," Cohen was quoted as saying in the Baldwin City *Signal.* Of course, the book was still available to read in the library. The issue was reading it out loud in class.

Three months later, Cohen had no qualms whatsoever about firing Santa on the basis of an unknown number of complaints, even if only one or two.

White thinks Stacy Cohen tried to apply pressure for him to be fired, or resign. "She didn't to my face. Although I had several e-mails that came from [other] people in the community that indicated I should resign." White has no solid evidence Cohen made efforts to have him removed, but it remains his suspicion.

The ACLU did not enter the case over the reading of passages from the book. White thought that was because the ACLU lawyer didn't want to see headlines that might have read ACLU SUES FOR GANG-RAPE READING IN CLASSROOM or something similar. Instead, they waited a few months and came after him over Santa. In either case, the underlying issue was his Christianity. "I believe there are still those people out there that are watching my every move," he said, "to make sure that I'm not doing something to push my religion or my fundamental beliefs on any kids. I think if I had to make another decision that was based on my values that we'd have people coming out of the out of the walls again.

"You have to understand that Douglas County is about as liberal as any place you'll find in America." As far as White is concerned, his problem is simply that the county he lives in is the Berkeley of the Plains. "We have a lot of those more liberal views that come from the University of Kansas and the Lawrence area. Of the 105 counties in Kansas, there was only one county in the last election that didn't vote for the president and vice president. And that was Douglas County."

White kept his job. Cohen says she was just trying to keep issues of religion evenhanded. "We're not inclusive of other religions," she said. "I don't see any of that other diversity coming home from school." And Cohen insisted that she wanted the schools not to ignore Christmas but to teach children about other religions and holidays as well.

About a year later Cohen left her job in the public relations department at Baker University, the first university established in Kansas. She moved to Lawrence and went back to teaching, taking a job as a roving instructor who visits schools to teach teachers.

White thinks she decided to move because of the book and

Santa controversies. "I think she thought that probably that her children would be better served if they were in schools in Lawrence, where the superintendent didn't ask teachers not to read this type of literature. And they can't have any Christmas references in the schools in Lawrence." Christmas is banned in the schools in Lawrence, Kansas, home of the University of Kansas.

The people who founded Baldwin City endured all the hardships of the pioneers everywhere in the American Midwest and West, and in addition they fought bloody battles over slavery and eventually triumphed in making Kansas a free state. They founded a university in a barren land barely able to support a country schoolhouse. They built a town and lived lives in harsh conditions on something more than secular dreams of prosperity. A year or so after the Santa episode, Daniel M. Lambert, Baker University president, called the university's founding "an astonishing act of faith" on the part of the intensely Christian pioneers who settled in the Baldwin City area during the 1850s.

Now an "act of faith" in Baldwin City was so astonishing it had to be stopped. Why? Evidently because parents might have to explain someone else's faith to their children. Superintendent White concluded the school board discussion of Santa's fate on that December evening by agreeing with Cohen that it was a good idea to notify parents of Santa's visit, but added that he thought it would be better if Santa did not visit the schools during Christmas 2003. Other board members agreed, and Santa was fired from Baldwin City (actually two Santas—after all, there were two Santa suits). "I was shocked when I was on the school board to learn the district owned *two* Santa suits. I doubt there are many schools that can claim that," Cohen wrote to the author. "Santa is not connected with any holiday but Christmas, which makes him a type of religious symbol."

That is, of course, exactly opposite the opinion of the United States Supreme Court. But Stacy Cohen felt perfectly confident about proceeding on the basis of her judgment instead of the high court's. By Cohen's reasoning, since Santa is connected to Christmas, and Christmas is connected to Christianity, and Christianity is not to be on display to the schoolchildren, the circle is therefore closed with Santa being forbidden.

Baker University is home to one of the world's largest collections of Bibles, five hundred of which are on permanent display. But kindergartners don't get near the Bible collection, and they did get near Santa.

Board member Ed Schulte helpfully suggested that the ACLU or other parents offer more information so the board could act on additional allegations of Christian impropriety contained in the ACLU letter. In addition to concern about Santa the ACLU had also alleged other unspecified violations of the constitutional separation of chuch and state. "We do want to take it seriously, we do want to be respectful, and we do want to do the right thing," he said. "We will try to follow up on any issues that come forward."

The curator of the Bible collection might have been quaking in fear. The ACLU walked away satisfied that a vague letter of protest, the publicity value of a name like "Sneaky Santa," and the fear of legal bombast could move mountains.

"I was shocked by how the Santa issue divided the community," Cohen wrote. "Some of our 'friendly' Christian residents left offensive messages on my answering machine. One said, 'F--- you and have a Merry Christmas.' It was nice when my family came home to find that a week before Christmas. Another woman told me I needed to turn on a Billy Graham special that evening because I was obviously a 'very, very sad person.'"

In Baldwin City schools both Santa and Stacy Cohen are gone. Neither is coming back. Superintendent White decided that Santa should remain out of the school classrooms until parents demanded his return. So far the community has remained silent on the subject of Santa, and Greg Childress, with his long white beard, his round belly, and his red suit, has not returned to the schools.

What happened to the two Santa suits the Baldwin City schools owned? "They're still hanging in the closet," said Superintendent White.

CHAPTER 4

PLANO, TEXAS:

A RED AND GREEN–FREE ZONE

Turning away from Kansas and toward Texas, where the toll in the skirmishing along the front lines of the war on Christmas claimed as victims the colors red and green. South and west of Baldwin City, just 513 miles, is a prosperous bedroom community of Dallas called Plano. Most people drive to Dallas to an office or a business, though Plano also brags a few megacorporations such as Frito-Lay, the chip (potato, not micro) company.

Plano seems placid at a glance, but beneath the surface Plano has been roiled by its own war on Christmas. It came to Plano, Texas, schools in December 2001, according to the parents involved. That was the year several of the parents whose children went to Plano elementary schools, a number of whom also happened to be members of a local church with a membership of close to twenty thousand, noticed that Christmas was being systematically scrubbed from them.

In December 2001 the Thomas Elementary school in Plano was getting ready to hold its annual winter party for students, a party that had taken the place of a traditional Christmas party for students at the end of the year, just before students took a break traditionally known as the Christmas break. In Plano the school district had discontinued the designation of that traditional break as Christmas out of deference to parents or students whose religion might not be Christian, or might not be any religion, and who might be offended or feel excluded by realizing they were participating in a Christian holiday—Christmas—they did not celebrate.

Plano is the largest city in Collin County, Texas, the ninth-fastest-growing county in the nation, according to U.S. Census estimates of 2004 (released April 2005). Plano added over thirty thousand new residents in 2004, which was an increase of 5.1 percent. These figures obviously indicate very rapid growth, and with that growth has come an increased expectation of racial or ethnic diversity from African Americans, Hispanics, and whites. But a more complicated ethnic diversity does not necessarily indicate growth in *religious* diversity. When it comes to religion, Collin County and Plano continue to reflect the national trends.

All of this makes it odd that Plano, Texas, of all places, would wage such a systematic war on Christmas in its public schools. But it happened, and because of the reasons given by the school district itself one can only conclude that the reason was hostility *to* or suspicion *of* Christians.

Back to the beginning.

December 2001, and Christmas is coming. One of the traditions in the Plano schools is that students exchange goodie bags at the annual winter party, formerly known as the Christmas party. Michaela Wade wanted to include in the goodie bags she gave out to her fellow students a pencil with words imprinted on it: Jesus Is The Reason For The Season.

In the same school, Thomas Elementary, another student,

Jonathan Morgan, wanted to pass out goodie bags that included
a candy cane–shaped pen to which was attached a laminated card
on which was printed a story called "The Legend of the Candy
Cane." This legend told a story about the candy cane that said it
was the invention of a candy maker who was a believer in Jesus
Christ, and that the candy cane is shaped like a J for Jesus, that its
colors represent the red of Christ's blood and white for purity,
and that it is hard candy because it represents the "rock" of
Christ.

Evidently there had been some experience with this sort of
thing before, because there was a policy in the Plano Independent
School District that no religious material of any kind could be ex-
changed or distributed on school grounds. Therefore, school principal Lynn Swanson had instructed her teachers to question (the
parents later used the word "interrogate") each student, and inspect each goodie bag to make certain that nothing of a religious
nature was being brought into the classroom.

According to the lawsuit later filed in federal court, Robin
Morgan, Jonathan's mother, specifically remembers being asked
by her son's teacher, Linda Ware, if there was anything religious
in Jonathan's goodie bag. Ware later recalled asking if there was
any "outside media" in the goodie bag, evidently referring to any
message that might have been printed or reproduced by a source
outside the school. Robin Morgan doesn't remember a question
that vague: She remembers Ware asking if there was anything religious in the bag.

Under this rule, Michaela's "Jesus Is The Reason" pencil and
Jonathan's "Legend of the Candy Cane" pens were confiscated
and Michaela and Jonathan were not allowed to give those gifts
to their classmates. School officials, according to a lawsuit filed

later, said the reason was the "religious viewpoint" message of the gifts. One student was not allowed to tell another student of his or her religious beliefs in the Plano schools.

In addition, the parents of both children noticed that while parents were asked to bring supplies and food to the winter party, they were also instructed that they should only bring white napkins, white paper plates and cups, and cakes and cupcakes should only be frosted in white. The rule was "white only." Red and green, the colors of Christmas, were not allowed.

Perhaps the most grating incident occurred when Bailey Wade, Michaela's sister, was told by her teachers that she could not say Merry Christmas. The occasion was a class project in which students were writing greeting cards to soldiers serving overseas in Iraq. Bailey and other students were told not to write Merry Christmas on the cards because it might "offend someone." Christine Wade found it difficult to explain to her daughters why the religious beliefs she had so carefully inculcated in her daughters were being treated by their school as something that should be shunned. What was wrong with saying Merry Christmas to someone? her daughters wanted to know. Christine said to me, "I told my daughters that the school wanted to appease everyone but Christians." How was someone offended if you offered a greeting that expressed your religious faith? And didn't we teach the children that Christians had an obligation to spread the word of Christianity? If that obligation were treated as an offense by the school, did that mean there was something wrong with spreading the word? Christine Wade began to feel it was not the school's right to create a conflict of conscience in her children or herself.

Christine Wade repeatedly asked the principal of her children's school, and officials in the district office, if it could possibly be true that all of these policies were being interpreted correctly? Was it true that her child could not give another child a pencil that had the name "Jesus" on it? Was it true that she—a parent—could not bring red and green napkins and cups and plates to the Christmas—(oooops)—*winter* party? Was it true that the children could not have a Christmas tree, or a Santa, or a reindeer in the school because they were symbols of the Christmas holiday? Was it true that the objections to the symbols of that holiday were that it was a Christian holiday? Yes, she was assured, it was all true. Those were the policies of the Plano Independent School District (PISD). No religion, no religious references of any sort were allowed. Certainly not if they were religious references made by a teacher to students, and to make certain the atmosphere was entirely secular, not even from one student to another.

In this regard, the Plano Independent School District was out of step with the Constitution of the United States as interpreted by the Supreme Court of the United States. The Bush Justice Department had sued a Massachusetts school district for trying to do exactly that—interfere with student-to-student communication—and even the ACLU had sided with the students. But no one at the Plano Independent School District seemed to know or care, and the policy was enforced in what was regarded elsewhere in the country as a clear violation of the law. The law was and is very clear: Student-to-student communication, even about religion, is free speech. Case closed.

Most everywhere, but not Plano, Texas. The school district had devised a policy, and it was strictly enforced, which required prior approval of the school principal—the government—for any written or spoken communication between students. That was the policy, but it was only enforced when the communication was about religion, and specifically about Christianity. Students, in fact, could receive communications about Little League baseball, or an invitation to a party from a friend, but nothing about religion, ever.

The next school year, 2002, was uneventful for both the Morgan and Wade families, in part because they were largely unaware of the fact that the law was on their sides. They submitted to the rules, so their children were not allowed to give gifts to their fellow students that reflected their religious beliefs, and while they were hurt and disappointed, they obeyed. The parents, Doug and Robin Morgan and Christine Wade, dutifully helped out with the winter party, but were annoyed that they were participating in a Christmas party that could not be called by its name. They realized that they—as Christians—embarrassed or caused resentment among the school officials, who insisted that they could not observe in the school, even in a secular way, a day that was very important to their faith.

Now instead of a non-Christian student or parent who felt uncomfortable or excluded in an overwhelmingly Christian atmosphere, Christians felt uncomfortable and excluded. They were being asked to celebrate something they didn't celebrate— winter—as if they were pagans in the Roman Empire. Everyone knew what was really being observed at that time of year, but no one was allowed to call it what it was: Christmas. When it came to the school a Christian's Christmas was unmentionable.

The Wade and Morgan families began to chafe at the idea that the school was so hostile to their religious beliefs that any symbols of the day were banned, including a tree, the singing of carols, the image of Santa Claus, even the colors red and green. It began to feel like they were being asked to reject all remnants of their religion at the school they supported with an enormous contribution in taxes, and where they allowed their children to be educated by people who were increasingly acting like strangers.

So two Christmas seasons passed and the Wades and the Morgans separately began to think that perhaps they did not want to continue cooperating in what was starting to feel like a betrayal of their firmly held faith. The 2003 Christmas season approached, and two of Plano's committed Christian families quietly decided enough was enough.

Meanwhile, across town another small anti-Christmas drama was unfolding with another student and another set of parents.

Michael and Kevin Shell were two years apart, and both attended the Wells Elementary school, one of forty elementary schools in Plano.

Fifty-two thousand students attended school in the Plano school district. It was a big school district, collecting over $4,000 a year in school taxes from the average-sized home valued at $234,100. Homes in Plano were often not average, however. It was quite possible, if not probable, to live in an upscale but common four-thousand-square-feet home with four bedrooms and four baths valued at $750,000 and find oneself paying $13,000 a year in school taxes. The Plano Independent School District in 2004 taxed homes and businesses, including Frito-Lay, Dr Pepper, computer giant EDS, and others, within its boundaries on a certified valuation of $28,571,480,374. At Plano's tax rate of $1.73 per $100 valuation, nearly half a billion dollars a year were collected from its taxpayers.

The parents of Michael and Kevin Shell began to think they were receiving disrespect in return.

Michael and Kevin Shell were interested in giving their friends a different kind of gift, but one that contained at its core a similar flaw as far as the school district was concerned. Michael and Kevin wanted to give friends tickets to events that both they and the school would classify as religious. They were tickets to events at a prominent Baptist church in the area, but in 2001 the schoolteachers for the boys did not object, and they were allowed to hand the tickets out to their friends, whether the friends wanted one or more.

Normally, "ticket" or "invitation" to a religious service might be seen by some as an aggrandizing description of what would otherwise be regarded as a come-on, a simple ruse to bring a person into a church so the faithful there could work their conversion magic. But this was different.

The Shell family, including Michael and Kevin, were members of a large Christian church in Plano, Texas, called the Prestonwood Baptist Church. If Dallas, Texas, is the buckle of the Bible Belt, as sometimes is said, Plano and the Prestonwood Baptist Church are the sparkling jewels set in that buckle. There is no bigger megachurch than Prestonwood Baptist. The church has 18,000 members. It is on 100 acres of land, and its construction budget was $80 million. It has an annual budget of $29 million, and it spends lavishly on its outreach and ministries. It has a 7,000-seat main church, which is not only an architectural marvel, but is a full state-of-the-art television studio.

Prestonwood's Christmas pageant features an orchestra of 75 musicians, a 450-voice choir, 500 actors, 50 dancers, flying angels, and a Noah's Ark that includes 6 sheep, 3 camels, 2 horses, and 2 donkeys on a stage three times larger than Radio City Music Hall's. Forty thousand people saw the production's 8 performances. Prestonwood Baptist Church puts on an enormous, hot-ticket event, and people who wish to attend had better make certain they have a ticket. Seldom if ever is there an empty seat.

Kevin and Michael's mother, Sunny, like many mothers was an active parent in her sons' school, and during the early part of 2003 noticed something in the school library she did not like. It was a book that dealt with puberty and child development issues. It also dealt with sex, and Sunny thought the book was a little too frank about sex for students her sons' ages.

Sunny Shell scheduled a meeting with the school principal, a woman named Lisa Long. She discussed her objections to the book and eventually prevailed on principal Long to remove the book from the library. Sunny Shell thought that was the end of it, but she was wrong.

The occasion was Easter 2003, arguably the holiest day on the Christian calendar, as it is the day Christians believe Jesus Christ rose from the dead and ascended to heaven. The Prestonwood Baptist Church was planning its Easter sunrise service not in its own seven-thousand-seat church in Plano but in the twenty-nine-thousand-seat ballpark at Frisco, the RoughRiders located in neighboring Frisco, Texas.

The Easter sunrise service for the Prestonwood Baptist Church was all that the Christmas pageant had delivered a few short months earlier, and even more.

Tickets were hard to come by, but Sunny had obtained a few dozen and offered them to Michael and Kevin to give away to their friends at school.

The event at the Ballpark at Frisco was meant to compete with other megaevents kids are lured to be part of—an alternative to rock concerts—and they were successful in that regard to a great degree. Plano, after all, is the town famous for its teenage suicides of the late 1980s, when the bedroom community of Dallas suffered nine over a few months. The community decided to act to stop the downward spiral of its children. One of the responses to that problem was the church, in particular the many Baptist and evangelical churches. The churches decided that they had to target kids too, the same as rock promoters and MTV. Michael and Kevin Shell were just the kind of kids the churches wanted: boys. Directing the behavior of young men in the full throes of puberty is always hard, but the churches have been willing to try.

Something was working. The teen suicide problem seemed to have largely gone away.

All of this leads back to Sunny Shell, the rather typical Plano mom trying to raise two boys right. She had them on physical activity schedules: They played soccer, baseball, and basketball. They wanted to play football, as every Texas boy does, but she was thinking about it.

Sunny wanted Michael and Kevin to be able to share the tickets and the experience with friends, for the simple reason that it meant other kids weren't trying to draw her sons off into some other activity that she might not like. And, of course, it was also important to Sunny, a follower of evangelical teachings, to spread the word of Christ. As was noted in a lawsuit later filed on behalf of Sunny and the others, Sunny Shell believed spreading the word of Jesus Christ is an obligation of the faith of every Christian.

As Easter approached Michael and Kevin wanted to give their tickets away. They wanted to make an announcement to their classmates that they had tickets and they were available, as they had in the past, but this time their teachers gave different answers. Michael was told he could offer tickets to his friends, but

Kevin's teacher, Suzie Snyder, said he would not be allowed to, since the tickets were religious.

Kevin asked where and when he could hand out the invitations. His teacher consulted with principal Lisa Long and the answer came back: "Never."

In fact, Kevin was told the tickets were "inappropriate material" for discussion at Wells Elementary school, and such materials could not be distributed by one student to another while on school property. Kevin could never discuss the tickets, such as what event one might see or hear if one used the ticket, nor could he distribute these tickets to his classmates in the school in the future. The boys went so far as to actually bring the tickets to school on April 7, 2003, and were once again given conflicting instructions. Michael could hand out tickets, Kevin could not.

The issue festered for another month. On May 2, both boys went to school with tickets to another event, a musical performance again staged at Prestonwood Baptist Church. Once again, it was a megaevent in the megachurch. Once again Michael was told he did have permission to give tickets to his classmates and Kevin did not.

Sunny Shell knew there was a problem: Why was Kevin being denied?

Sunny Shell confronted Principal Long, who said she would investigate and report back. Sunny Shell now called the president of the school board, Mary Beth King, and demanded an explanation in a voice-mail message. A few days later Sunny Shell got a call from a PISD administrator named Carole Greisdorf, who explained it was Michael's teacher who was wrong. It was Michael's teacher who had been taken into conference and informed that the policy of the Plano Independent School District was that no religious material could be distributed on school grounds during school hours, ever.

Sunny Shell requested a confirmation from the school district that the policy was being correctly implemented. After all, she saw other organizations distributing information to children in the school. It was common to hear from the Boy or Girl Scouts, or from sports teams that were organizing in the schools. What was wrong with Micheal and Kevin sharing tickets to a big event, tickets that were in fact hard for anybody to get?

Greisdorf even told Sunny Shell that Michael and Kevin could not distribute the tickets at lunch or recess because those periods of time were considered curriculum. Later, Michael and Kevin's lawyer asked to see the boys' grades for recess and lunch, and of course there were none. Lunch and recess were no more part of the curriculum than what they did on the school bus on the ride home. It was a ruse to wall off the school from Christians and their Christmas at every turn.

Now Sunny Shell, like the Morgans and Christine Wade before her, was starting to get the idea that the doctrine of separation of church and state was being used in Plano, Texas, as a method to carry out hostility against her religion and the religion of her children. Her children were taught to spread the word of God, not by force or by coercion, but by simply offering the word. If that aspect of the faith were forbidden, was it not outright hostility to her faith?

As far as the school district was concerned, the problem was over for the moment. Sunny Shell got an e-mail from the school district's outside law firm promising an e-mail explanation in the future. But nothing ever came.

For the Morgan family the issue came to a head in December

2003, as the school prepared for yet another winter party. Jonathan Morgan again wanted to include in his goodie bag a pen in the shape and color of a candy cane and a laminated card attached on which would be printed "The Legend of the Candy Cane." By this time Doug Morgan, Jonathan's father, knew there was going to be trouble over the candy cane, and he also knew that Assistant Superintendent Carole Greisdorf was handling the problem at district headquarters. Morgan called and asked for an appointment with Greisdorf. She called back and referred him to the Thomas School principal, Lynn Swanson.

A meeting was set for December 4, 2003. Christine Wade also wanted to come, but Swanson refused to allow her in the meeting. Instead, it was Doug and Robin Morgan, and Jonathan's grandparents, Rod and Ramona Shafer, Robin's mother and father.

It was a contentious meeting. Doug and Robin had issues and laid them out for Swanson in a list:

1. Students were told they could not say Merry Christmas and should say happy holidays instead.
2. Students and parents were being interrogated about religious items in the childrens' goodie bags, and if found they were confiscated.
3. School officials insisted on calling the end-of-year school break "winter" and forbade use of the word "Christmas."
4. School officials imposed rules on the winter break parties that forbade the use of any materials, including plates, cups, and napkins, that might suggest or symbolize Christmas, including the colors red or green.
5. Bailey Wade had been told he could not write Merry Christmas on greeting cards sent to soldiers serving overseas.

6. Parents were constantly being told if they wanted their son or daughter to express his or her religion in school they should send him or her to a religious school.

Turning aside these complaints, the principal told the Morgans and Shafers that the winter party was to be entirely secular, and any symbol or communication of a religious nature was forbidden. Doug and Robin Morgan left the meeting in a state of disbelief. It did not seem possible that such outright hostility to their religion could be official policy.

A few days later Doug Morgan sent an e-mail to Assistant Superintendent Greisdorf, saying his son wanted to distribute a gift to his classmates that included a "religious viewpoint" item, the candy cane and the legend. Morgan wanted to know if Swanson's interpretation of PISD policy was correct. Greisdorf responded the same day, within an hour actually, that Swanson had gotten the policy "exactly right."

The day of the party came, and the Morgans had decided to press the issue. They arrived carrying Jonathan's goodie bags with the candy canes and the legends inside them. They asked to see Swanson, but she was unavailable.

Doug and Robin Morgan proceeded to Jonathan's classroom and put the tray of goodie bags outside the classroom door, on the floor. The teacher, Mrs. Helmke, had said that Jonathan could not bring the tray in the classroom but had to take it to the library and place it on a special table, in accordance with a new district policy on the distribution of off-campus material. She said that if the bags contained any religious material they could not enter the classroom. They had to be distributed through the library. That day the Morgans took the bags home.

Other students had goodie bags in the classroom. The party began, parents in attendance. Doug Morgan was also told he could not give the legend card to other parents.

The teacher's gift to her students was a pencil with a snowman image on it.

All the students gave gifts to their friends. Except Jonathan. His goodie bags were treated as if they were radioactive, forbidden in the classroom, sent to another room—the library—some distance down a long hollow hallway from the classroom.

At the same time, the Shell boys, Michael and Kevin, were attending a new school, Hughston Elementary. After the Christmas break from school, early in the year, Sunny Shell wrote to administrator Greisdorf saying that Michael and Kevin were back in the ticket game and wanted to offer their classmates tickets to an event at Prestonwood Baptist Church called the "Harvest Rally."

The Harvest Rally was another big event in the classic style of a Prestonwood megaoccasion. It certainly promised to be entertaining, if for no other reasons than its top-tier professional staging and production.

Michael, now a fifth grader, and Kevin, now a third grader, had one hundred free tickets to give to their classmates and friends. Greisdorf referred Sunny Shell to their school's principal, Luanne Collins, and they met on January 22, 2004. She asked that Michael and Kevin be allowed to hand out tickets during noninstructional times in a nondisruptive manner.

Collins said that PISD policy was that the boys would never be permitted to distribute religious content material, nor would they be allowed to make any verbal announcements during either class or recess.

When Shell wrote to Superintendent of Schools Douglas Otto

she was informed that the policy on distribution of material from student to student had changed somewhat. The new rule required that students place anything they wanted distributed on an information table designated by the principal of the school. This was a rule designed to control the free expression of Christianity by her children, and Sunny Shell now realized that the problem Christians were having with the Plano Independent School District was going to have to be solved by a judge.

Tensions had now been building for three years, and into this gathering storm walked the person of Sherrie Versher, another mom in Plano active in her church. Her daughter Stephanie went to Rasor Elementary school in the 2003–2004 school year.

Sherrie Versher had become troubled when she heard her daughter had been disciplined at school for giving tickets to her friends to see a drama about the Crucifixion of Christ. Mel Gibson's movie, *The Passion of The Christ*, was in the news; her friends were interested.

Principal Jackie Bomchill heard about Stephanie's discussion with her friends, and that Stephanie had actually given some tickets to her classmates. Bomchill ordered Stephanie and the friends questioned, and she demanded the return of any tickets Stephanie had given the friends. When she had collected all the tickets Stephanie had given out, she threw them away. Stephanie's teacher was instructed to tell the girl she was not allowed to give tickets to her friends that involved a religious event.

About this time, Stephanie's half birthday was coming up.

At ten and a half years old, Stephanie was in the fifth grade. She was active in socializing, as are many girls her age, and she was planning to celebrate her half birthday with a few of her friends and classmates in the cafeteria at the end of the lunch hour on January 16, 2004. The custom at this school was to allow students whose birthdays fell in the summer to celebrate a half birthday during the school year when the birthday student and his or her classmates were all together. Students whose birthdays fell during the school year were allowed this small consideration on their traditional birthdays, so why not the kids whose birthdays unluckily fell during the summer break?

And it was the custom for the mother to bring a tray of snacks, brownies or such, along with a small gift for each of the classmates. They would all be gathered at a table in the cafeteria for a few minutes at the end of the lunch period. The mother would bring in the tray of snacks, each classmate would get a brownie and a gift, such as a pencil, a plastic ring, or a key chain, the party would be over when the bell rang, and everybody would proceed to their classroom. The inherent exclusivity of a party that included only one class was made up for by the fact that everybody was allowed to have such small parties.

Sherrie Versher knew there could be trouble over the gifts she planned to attach to the twenty-four wrapped brownies. She and her daughter Stephanie had chosen two pencils: One was colored brightly and had the word "Moon" imprinted in the wood; the second was printed with the words "Jesus Loves Me This I Know Because The Bible Tells Me So."

Sherrie Versher made an appointment with the principal of Rasor Elementary, Jackie Bomchill. Versher was informed that the gift could include the pencil with the word "Moon" but not the pencil that carried the long phrase that began with the words "Jesus Loves Me."

The rule was so clearly aimed at suppressing a Christian message that Versher wanted to make certain she was understanding the administrator correctly. She said she could not believe that her daughter could give away one pencil with the word "Moon" on it and not a pencil with the word "Jesus" on it. Had she caught the school preferring pagans over monotheists? Certainly the idea of a moon worshipper might be more threatening than the idea of a Christian, she thought. But she soon began to feel that the school district did not share her view. She requested a clarification of the policy and received a call from an assistant to the superintendent of schools. The administrator confirmed that indeed the school district policy was that no material, not even a gift from one student to another, could contain any religious references. It was not legal, technically, for one student to speak to another in the written word if the subject was God. It was a very simple rule. No God.

Versher took the Jesus pencil off each of the twenty-four wrapped brownies and put the handful of pencils in her purse. She then walked down the hallway toward the cafeteria, where her daughter and classmates were waiting for their party, and as she walked, fuming still over her confrontation with the school officials, she said in her lawsuit she "muttered" to herself, "Satan is in the building."

School officials did not regard Sherrie's vocalizing as muttering. They heard her shouting, and they became alarmed. School officer John Beasley followed Sherrie down the hallway to the cafeteria. When Sherrie arrived at her daughter's table there was approximately five minutes left in the lunch period to have Stephanie's party. Beasley was standing nearby talking on a cell phone. It has since been learned in court proceedings he was speaking with the Plano Police Department.

Stephanie asked where the Jesus pencils were, and her mother, Sherrie, said she would only be allowed to give those pencils to her friends outside the school building. One of the classmates, a fifth grader, said this was the same as "the candy cane issue."

The bell rang and the students headed for class. Walking to Stephanie's locker Sherrie Versher gave her daughter the Jesus pencils and told her to keep them in her backpack, and to give them to her friends after school and outside. She warned her more than once to not remove the pencils from her backpack until after school.

The lawsuit alleges Sherrie then continued on to the wing of the building where her second daughter was in class, "to check on her," and asked Officer Beasley why he was following her. Beasley said he was escorting her out of the building, and "the police are on their way." Beasley said Versher was making threats and creating a disturbance.

Sherrie left the school, noticing two police cars had arrived. She drove off the school property, and a short distance down the road was stopped by the police car that had followed her. The officers asked her if she had made a threat, and she said she had not made a threat, but while speaking to herself had said the words "Satan is in the building." The cops checked her license, said, "No problem," and she continued on her way home.

After school she walked back to the school to pick up her daughters. As she approached she saw Stephanie on the lawn with her friends, handing out the Jesus pencils. Principal Jackie Bomchill suddenly appeared. She took the pencils back from the friends, took those Stephanie still held, and scolded Stephanie, telling her that she was in violation of PISD policy, and that she was not allowed to give out "those Christian pencils" on school property. Again, this sequence of events was alleged by Versher and other parents in a federal lawsuit.

Bomchill and Beasley then turned to Sherrie, who had just arrived, telling her that if Stephanie was caught giving out Christian tickets or Jesus pencils again while on school property she would be kicked out of school. They also accused Sherrie of being "purposely defiant" because Bomchill insisted that she had told Sherrie that Stephanie could only give away the pencils off school property, across the street. Sherrie insisted Bomchill had said "outside the building." Beasley cracked that Sherrie "apparently had a hearing problem and should have it checked," according to the lawsuit in which the Vershers were plaintiffs.

Sherrie said they continued to harass her as she was leaving the school grounds, and for the following week as she escorted her kids to and from school she was stalked by school officers; a police car was stationed on campus until she left.

The only incident, according to Sherrie Versher and her attorneys, in which Bomchill and the Plano Independent School District prohibited the distribution of a gift at a Rasor Elementary school student party or gathering was during the school year that Stephanie's Jesus pencil was barred, forbidden to cross any farther than the curb at the street in front of the school.

When the Morgans, the Wades, the Shells, and the Vershers sued in federal court the pleadings said that it is their "sincerely held religious faith and Christian belief that Christians are commanded by the Bible and Holy Scripture to engage in person to person communication of religious viewpoint messages through the spoken word and through the sharing of religious viewpoint materials in an effort to introduce those with whom they are associated to the truth of the Christian faith and the gospel of Jesus Christ."

The school district took many months to craft an answer to the plaintiffs' lawsuit. Its attorney, Richard Abernathy, said the lawsuit was about nothing more than the "desire of a few adults to proselytize their religion in the public schools amongst very young children." The superintendent of schools, Doug Otto, spoke out through a news release that the district had devised a series of policy changes designed to settle the lawsuit. He said it was his job to preserve the neutral setting of the school for "people of faith, and people of non-faith." Therefore, the school district's policies were correct.

But by this equation it was obvious that in a contest between faith and nonfaith the neutral position at Plano is always nonfaith. Consequently, it was obvious that the school district was hostile to religion, in that it had devised a system in which *nonfaith* is unfairly favored to prevail over faith. In its efforts to protect nonbelievers from believers the government had become an opponent of believers. In violation of the Constitution the government, PISD, had rigged the game by defining the ideal outcome as a world of schools in which there was no mention of anything with a religious connection at all, which is declared to be the religion-neutral position. It is in fact the nonfaith position, and the nonfaith outcome. Dr. Douglas Otto unfairly favored nonfaith and disfavored faith.

CHAPTER 5

EUGENE, OREGON:

"THEREFORE, WE DECIDED TO BAN THEM"

The story of how Christmas trees came to be banned in the city of Eugene's municipal offices is the tale of a timber town that was swallowed whole by the culture of a major university, a culture based on the beliefs of ecopreservationists and antiindustrialists and the corresponding decline of an older way of life, an economy based on cutting big trees. In the new Eugene, the Christmas tree was suspect because the campus ethic of diversity had crept into city hall and otherwise sensible people were so disconnected from a reality others call normal that it seemed to be nothing more than routine for the city manager to wake up one morning and decide to impose a ban on Christmas trees.

It was a decision he came to regret fast, but it was a predictable situation because of what Eugene, Oregon, had become.

Eugene is a place that was known in the past as the lumber capital of the world, and now probably still is a big player, but not a world beater.

"It was a different era. When you look back fifty years ago, it was a different industry. That was the days of big timber and big mills and Paul Bunyan, and logs coming down the river. I mean, it was real romantic. And we romanticize those days."

Speaking with Tom Colct, who is a manager with Westwood Lumber, one of the few lumber mills to remain in Eugene, a listener can almost see it. A mill town bustled and roared; a university town is quiet and leafy. Fifty years ago, when timber was king, there were over 150 mills in Eugene and Lane County. Now there are only eleven in the county and fewer still—four—in Eugene itself. Meanwhile, the University of Oregon campus has grown enormous: from 7,470 students and 637 employees in 1950, in 2004 it topped out at 20,339 students and 5,645 employees.

But more than sheer numbers is the obvious cultural victory of the campus over the extraction industries: Lumber employs far fewer people than in the past, and the concerns of academics and university people has spread off the campus and into the city, especially city hall.

The loggers have known for decades that they lost. What went with them was the everyday common sense of the logging industry, and what replaced it was the airy ecothinking of the university. As the new millenium approached, the University of Oregon and the city of Eugene were consumed with diversity, the new watchword. The clash of a chain-saw culture based on logging and wood products with a university campus outraged by privateering on public lands and armed with an environmental law center to fight back produced the usual result: Professors always trump loggers.

"Somewhere around sixty percent of the votes in Oregon are between Eugene and Portland. And they are more or less urban," lumberman Colet says. "So the poor folks that live out in the rural areas who might need to log for a living or work in a sawmill, or . . . or run cattle, or . . . do whatever you do, it doesn't matter what they want. They're gonna be outvoted, outgunned by the politics of urban progressive politics."

At best the loggers have learned to coexist with an overbearing and overwhelming liberal university force, but it is a wary stalemate between vast dimunition on the side of the timber industry and self-satisfied triumphalism on the part of the ecoacademics of the campus.

Believe it or not, the slow but inexorable conquest of the city by the campus ultimately explains why the city of Eugene, Oregon, got out of bed one morning to read worldwide headlines describing it as the town that banned Christmas trees.

It started with the demise of the timber industry worker and the culture that went with physical labor in Eugene. At the high-water mark of Eugene's timber industry, when the 150 sawmills and plywood plants belched steam and smoke and employed thousands of people in Lane County, Oregon, the university had little power to insist on change among the lumber barons or their workers. Lumber was the dominant culture.

Time solved that problem: Two generations of activists from the environmental program of the law school of the University of Oregon and the job-killing efficiencies of modern wood-processing technologies vastly reduced the number of mills to less than a dozen and cut the employment rolls to a tenth of what they once were. The industry still produces the same amount of plywood as ever, and cuts more timber than anywhere else in the timber-rich Pacific Northwest, but its influence in the community has waned in the same proportion as the number of lost workers. It is the absent voter who once worked in the timber industry, and who has now moved on, who has really determined the atmosphere and culture of the contemporary community of Eugene, Oregon. Earl Weaver, the great manager of the Baltimore Orioles baseball team, called this phenomenon "addition by subtraction."

The liberal arts–based University of Oregon in Eugene produces few, if any, defenders of the area's historic timber industry. Instead, its liberal-minded students and professors and its environmental law activists have worked to restrain the industry under the notions of preserving the resource and sustainable growth and, frankly, the campus cry "Save Our Forests."

All this leads to the doorstep of Eugene's city hall. The lumberman's basic problem—the university attitude about the wood products industry—had also invaded the city government of Eugene, where an echo chamber debate on diversity among employee committees produced a casually and thoughtlessly disastrous decision.

A window on the problem: In the State of the City address she delivered the first working day of 2005, Mayor Kitty Piercy introduced her economic proposals by quoting David Gottfried of the U.S. World Green Building Council: "'How can we afford not to understand and embody standard practices that provide good air quality, energy and water efficiency, and health and comfort for all?'"

Nice, but what does that have to do with Eugene's local industries, which the mayor is charged with improving?

The mayor quoted Gottfried again: "'Adoption of these natural principles will improve your firm's bottom line, ensure the survival of the planet, and contribute toward your own personal contentment.'"

Primitives in this school of thought might have referred to this policy as "holistic." Coming from the chief executive of the city government, it might have sounded a lot more like, "If you do it our way, you will save the world and we won't make you feel guilty."

"Furthermore, in my conversations with people throughout our community," the mayor continued, "I have learned that across all sectors and political affiliations, our residents believe Eugene can and should have a strong economy and protect this beautiful natural environment." In Eugene the logging culture, the sawmill-on-every-corner era, the traffic dominated by big trucks hauling big trees—it was gone, and the attitude, barely concealed below the surface, was good riddance.

"People choose to live here because they love the rivers, ridges, and trees, the greenness of our valley, the clean water and air," the mayor enthused in her address. "They also want good employment opportunities and a strong economy, so they can raise their families. By encouraging businesses that are sustainable, we can meet the goals of environmental regeneration, social equity, and profitability," Mayor Piercy said.

Of Oregon's 150 largest businesses, just 17 are located in Eugene, and most are found below number 117.

In 1951, Lane County, Oregon, was home to 179 sawmills, with 39 in Eugene's city limits. Imagine! Thirty-nine log ponds. Thirty-nine wigmam sawdust burners. Thirty-nine destinations for big rigs on the town streets loaded with thousands of tons of logs.

A little more than half a century later only 23 wood-products companies are in the top 150 companies in the entire state of Oregon, and of that only 4 are in Eugene.

The biggest employer in the city of Eugene, by far, is the University of Oregon.

The mayor boasted that she participates in the area's Growth and Development Roundtable, which is made up of sixteen community members, including developers, building owners, businesspeople, and municipal planners, and the timber industry was not mentioned by name. It has become a small, perhaps politically insignificant feature of the social landscape of Eugene.

This is a city government that cannot bring itself to mention the timber industry but has enormous bureaucratic energy for issues like invasive plant species. The city, in fact, has issued a policy on the planting of invasive species and issued a list of forty-one plants that city workers are prohibited from planting on city property and a companion list of seventeen plants that are permitted but highly discouraged, and a third list of sixty-nine other plant species that are acceptable alternatives to those on the prohibited or discouraged lists.

With the timber industry in a box, city employees have the time and inclination to import notions such as invasive species control directly from the campus. One of the other issues straight off the campus was diversity.

Eugene is a city seemingly obsessed with diversity issues, almost as if it were desperate to have diversity issues. Eugene might be one of the most nondiverse cities in the nation. It is 93.7 percent white; it is home to twice as many Hispanics as either Asians or American Indians. The percentage of African Americans is tiny, much below national population levels.

But Eugene wanted diversity to be an issue. Or at least, its city manager did.

"One of the things that we were very deeply involved in is a program to recognize and support diversity efforts in the organization," said Jim Johnson, the former city manager of the city of Eugene in an interview with me. "That is, the community in general doesn't have a lot of minorities, but the minority groups are growing. And so we wanted to do a better job of reflecting in hiring and in support of those minority groups within the organization."

Jim Johnson asked various employee groups to form diversity committees and subcommittees, and asked them to work on diversity issues and report back. Diversity committees begat more diversity committees inside Eugene city hall.

"So we started a very large effort of diversity. Programming of diversity issues, discussions, each department within the city was asked to develop a diversity plan, each department had its own diversity committee. So there was an organizationwide diversity committee also, and a representative from each department came in and discussed, reported to this larger committee about what they were doing."

But it was out of these near endless meetings and discussions of a diversitopia in the city of Eugene that the topic eventually turned to Christmas and Christians. And it turned out that some people in Eugene were not as tolerant as a university town might be expected to be. "As a part of that I started to have some discussions about holidays. And a subgroup of people started to discuss holiday decorations and . . . came to me eventually and said, 'There's a number of people in the organization who really do not like, they are upset with, holiday decorations that are of Christian origin.'"

Should a diversity officer trained to stomp out intolerance have heard alarm bells ringing? Some might think so, but not in Eugene.

"And they focused a lot on Christmas trees. To them it was very much a nonsecular kind of symbol, and they thought it reminded them too much of Christianity."

Jim Johnson is a mild-mannered middle-aged father and husband whose profession is municipal administration. He's been a county chief administrative officer. He's been a city manager in several Oregon cities. Yet somehow this admission of anti-Christian discrimination right off the bat from a group of his city employees didn't sound any alarms. A group of his employees stood in front of him and said they didn't like symbols of Christianity, and one might assume that they didn't like actual Christians either, and they wanted him to act in his official capacity in furtherance of their bias.

He took the request under consideration.

In the municipal system used in Eugene, Oregon, the city manager is a position of wide-ranging discretion and power. In this system, the city manager makes decisions. If his decisions are unpopular enough with the city council and the mayor, they can replace him or her, but that seldom happens. Most city managers can survive all manner of small disasters: mistaken judgment, unforeseen events, even costly litigation.

Jim Johnson is no longer the city manager in Eugene, Oregon, and he said it has nothing to do with what happened to the Christmas trees, and that may be true. He reached early retirement age, took his pension, and makes a nice retirement living as a freelance city manager for any community that finds itself without a city manager and needs someone on an interim basis. But it is also true that the mistake he was about to make would have cost most city managers their jobs, if not immediately, then eventually, when the affair and controversy had died down.

Johnson's human resources manager was also involved. His name is Lauren Chiounard, a twenty-seven-year resident of Eugene, with twenty-four years as a city official. Chiounard had an assistant and a small staff. Their job was to investigate situations and make recommendations to the city manager.

"Over the years, come Christmastime, we would see a certain amount of Christmas trees going up in lobbies, our public lobbies. For instance, I have a public lobby where people come in to look for jobs. So they're filling out job applications, that sort of thing." Chiounard speaks in an energetic and enthusiastic manner, and he recounted the incident in detail. I interviewed Chiounard in the spring of 2005, five years after the incident. "In part, they are people's [employees'] work space, but they're also an extension of the public's ability to come in and connect with us. So across the organization, Christmas trees as a normal course were up in many public lobbies around Christmastime."

A remarkable process was beginning in the diversity corridors of the city of Eugene: the targeting of Christmas and Christians by the city government under the banner of diversity. But in its very bluntness this policy of anti-Christian bias was unique. Certainly if it were the same bias at work with another group, the policy and the thinking that went into it would be immediately denounced, most loudly perhaps by these very members of the diversity committees.

"We started to realize that there was a certain segment of our employees that really felt a little put out by having to deal with Christmas trees. Because it wasn't part of their culture. And it wasn't part of their upbringing. And they felt like, 'You know what? We don't really mind if somebody has a little something in their office or something like that, 'cause that's their private office and that's their private space. But is it really appropriate for us to be putting up Christmas trees in lobbies, in public lobbies and in public places across the organization?' And we were getting a certain level of complaints from community members saying, 'What is this? Is this a Christian organization?'"

Couldn't have that.

"So then we started to have this debate about, 'Well, is a Christmas tree a secular symbol? Or is it a religious symbol?' And that was a very fascinating debate. And we decided that, you know, indeed, you could say it's a secular symbol. But realistically—it's a religious symbol. It's a Christian symbol in some ways—although it was stolen from the pagans, from my research on it."

Here the diversity committees of the city of Eugene decided to ignore the dictates of the Supreme Court of the United States, which has found that the Christmas tree is a secular symbol, not a religious symbol. The court had decided, but no matter to Chiounard and his staff. "So we decided, 'You know what? Let's just make one more step further here and decide that we're going to say it's *not* okay to have Christmas trees in public spaces, put up by employees or by the organization in public spaces.'

"We made some new rules and said, 'We're no longer gonna have Christmas trees in city facilities unless it's in your own private office and you wanna put up some decoration like that.' Just like if I wanted to have a cross, a Christian cross in my office, or a sign that says I LOVE JESUS. I could have that in my office right now."

But not out in the open, not a Christmas tree. Chiounard's staff and the employee diversity committees fashioned a recommendation to City Manager Jim Johnson. No one thought it would ever attract much notice, except perhaps a few good reviews in the diversity industry journals and Web sites.

"So we decided," Chiounard said, in his urgent tone, "'You know what, there's enough people that really do feel strongly that this is a Christian symbol, and that it is an artifact of a Christian holiday even if it's not a Christian symbol, so to speak.' It's an artifact of a Christian holiday."

He paused. "Therefore, we decided we would ban them."

Of course, the diversity committees, even Lauren Chiounard, the human resources manager, could not just make the change. All they could do was report and recommend. For a Christmas tree ban to become policy, one other person had to take official action. They had to convince City Manager Jim Johnson. I interviewed Johnson at length in early 2005.

"So what they said was," Johnson recalled, "'Mr. City Manager, Jim, will you consider, in the workplace, asking people not to put up Christmas trees—that symbol of that birth of Christ? And why don't you instead just have kind of a variety of holiday decorations, but they can be seasonal, they can be any number of things, just not this symbol which everybody has in their house, and which is a symbol of the birth of Christ.'"

A little reading would reveal that the tree is a Norse symbol that goes back thousands of years, predating Christianity by several millennia. It was adopted as a Christmas holiday symbol by

Germans, most likely beginning with Martin Luther. It was re-
vived as a Christmas symbol in America in the early 1800s. It is a
symbol of a family gathering at Christmastime, but credible
scholars do not argue that it is a symbol of the birth of Christ.

Johnson had diversity on his mind too. "Of our thirteen hundred employees we had a lot of people who were interested in
diversity issues. And so I decided to make it my legacy to the organization to support these efforts and to help them flourish
within the organization." Diversity was to be Johnson's *legacy.* "So
I considered it, I talked about it, listened to people on both sides,
and so forth. And eventually I put that policy into place, again as
part of that diversity effort."

Jim Johnson may not have been the first, but he was certainly
one of the very first officials to ban Christmas trees from public
view in publicly owned places, declaring it was because Christmas meant Christianity. There is a reason he was the first, or one
of the first: It is patently illegal. Hostility to religion is as unconstitutional as official establishment of religion, and here the city
of Eugene was taking steps that officially targeted and discriminated against Christians.

Christians made people uncomfortable in Eugene.

Under this proposed change of official city policy, Christmas
trees were to be banned in certain public places owned and controlled by the city of Eugene. Jim Johnson did not regard the policy as particularly remarkable. And neither did Lauren Chiounard.
Of course, they were both wrong.

"It was, I thought, a carefully worded policy that explained
why we were doing it, and set out some guidelines for departments that said, 'We would prefer that . . .' and, in fact, it told

them, 'You cannot put up a Christmas tree on public property within the city government, fire stations, City Hall, and so forth.'" Johnson was satisfied that it was a wise decision.

If Christmas trees were already up, they had to come down. If they weren't up yet, they had to stay down. The Christmas tree ban was in effect with Jim Johnson's signature on a piece of paper. It was the first December of the new millennium, and the city of Eugene was suddenly the capital of anti-Christmas forces: It had banned Christmas trees.

What happened then?

"There were a number of people who were upset with the policy, both within the organization [and] in the community," Johnson said.

Chiounard put it differently: "And then all hell breaks loose."

The local paper, the Eugene *Register Guard,* reported heavily on the new rule, pouring on the scorn in both the editorial and opinion pages. The *Wall Street Journal* picked up the item and ran a mocking, scolding column condemning the grinches in Eugene's city hall. And the whole thing had Jim Johnson's name on it. The calls came to him.

"Then, literally, it went international," Johnson said, looking back. "That is, the BBC picked it up, probably from wire service reports within the United States. And so I was handling phone calls from the British press about this policy." And the story rocketed around the world on the BBC's international services: American city bans Christmas trees!

Was it a first? Johnson was chagrined to admit it might have been. "It's close, it was certainly groundbreaking, it was certainly ahead of the curve."

Did Jim Johnson ever intend to be leading the way in an attack on Christmas trees in America? "Absolutely not."

But he was.

"It was generally misunderstood," Johnson said in his own defense five years later. "Generally, it was thought that I was banning Christmas trees in the community as a whole. They didn't quite understand that we're a public agency, and it was internal policy to the organization. It had nothing to do with the community as a whole."

But it did. The firemen objected early and loudly. They couldn't put up a Christmas tree in the firehouse, and firemen have friends in the media. The press coverage was relentless, and it was all aimed at Jim Johnson, not Lauren Chiounard. But Chiounard took it personally. "So then we started getting just real bad press. And I mean, the press went all the way to Europe on this thing. And, of course, you know, to a certain degree people tried to make us a laughingstock, which to me was very offensive," Chiounard said, still smarting after half a decade. "But it was such a fascinating experiment to see the public lashing out at us, people trying to make us look like fools and idiots—people saying we have taken PC way too far."

It wasn't quite so fascinating for Jim Johnson. To this day the city manager's office keeps a thick three-ring binder with all of the letters sent to Johnson while the battle raged. Numbering in the thousands, a few were supportive, but most were vicious, some even threatening.

In Eugene, the hometown of the University of Oregon Ducks, one liquor store owner changed the sign on the outside reader board to say: "Go Ducks, and take Jim Johnson with you."

"In fact, it affected me quite a bit. I was very concerned for my personal safety," Johnson said. "I received a telephone threat, which the police responded to, came up to my house." The difficulty was that while Johnson was receiving vague but ominous threats to himself and his family and his home, he was not there to help protect his family. He was out of town, in Boston attending a convention of city managers. "So the police officer showed up at my door and talked to my wife about the threat." The police increased the patrols around the Johnson home, and nothing came of it. But Johnson's wife and family decamped to Portland for a few days, just in case.

The experience, understandably, rattled the Johnson household.

And what did Johnson's friends say?

"They asked, 'Why?' They were a bit surprised."

Chiounard may not have been the person who made the decision, but he was quoted widely in the media, staunchly defending the decision. "We even had some people who were not Christians who felt like, 'You know, I was raised in a family where we had Christmas trees anyways, and it is secular. I don't know why you're making such a big deal.' So, we got it from both sides," Chiounard recalled.

"What we were doing was saying, 'We're gonna take a forward stance on being more of an inclusive organization.' And if we felt like there was a certain segment of our population that was being offended—and that's a tough word for a lot of people who are into Christmas trees to understand—but some of these folks were Jewish folks and others who just found the whole Christmas holiday season an offensive assault on them.

"When we got that many people saying, 'This is really offensive. It's one thing to have to walk into a shopping mall and get hit with a Christmas tree. But when we have to come to work and see the same symbol over and over? Can't we have some peace?'"

Chiounard's voice perked up at the prospect. "And we went, 'You know what? We're with you.'"

Back in Jim Johnson's office it was becoming clear to him that the one expert missing from his advisory diversity committees was a lawyer. Had Johnson consulted at all with an attorney to find out where the Supreme Court was on this issue for any simple guidance?

"That is exactly why in 2001 the policy changed," he told me in our interview.

The policy changed back? "Yes, it did. We changed the policy in the next year, primarily because I did more reading of the legal issues associated with it. It became very clear that the Supreme Court does not believe that a Christmas tree in and of itself is a Christian symbol."

In other words, after making the decision Johnson finally consulted the records of the United States Supreme Court to investigate what the law said about Christmas, and about Christmas trees in particular. What he discovered was that everything that had gone before, all the diversity meetings, the recommendations, was conducted in ignorance of the law. And the Christmas tree ban itself was just plainly illegal. No basis in the law. With growing dismay Johnson read the opinions of the justices of the Supreme Court and learned conclusively that the state of the law in the United States is that the Christmas tree is a secular symbol. Period. No matter how much city officials may want to declare it otherwise, it was simply not a religious symbol under the law, even if Christian believers and various nonbelievers think it is.

Even the anti-Christmas forces readily admit it. Albert J. Menendez, who has written several books arguing against Christian influence in the schools, has also written extensively on the use of trees as symbols that predate Christianity by thousands of years. Some primitive impulses remain even in the modern human, he reported, and decorated trees is one.

Johnson read the law with a growing sense that he had been led down the garden path by an earnest group of people who were simply wrong. And so, did Johnson feel at all *had* by the people who had convinced him that they were recommending the right course?

In my interview, for the first time Johnson admitted that yes, indeed, he did feel that his friends had betrayed him by leading him into such a blatantly illegal position. Even though it had been his responsibility to read the law before implementing a new rule, and neglecting that was his own personal failure, he felt burned. "I would say I did have some concerns that I had accepted advice and was listening to heartfelt comments that were probably more individual to those people, and to the groups that they represented, and may not have been based on the law."

This news shocked Chiounard.

"We did look at the law ahead of time. And we concluded—and I'm talking [about] me and my staff and who are, you know, somewhat responsible if Jim feels let down and, and trust me, I know Jim really well. So I'm not saying anything bad about Jim. But if he felt like we let him down . . . ," Chiounard's voice trailed off.

"But I'm willing to take part of this, because I was his adviser on this thing throughout—myself and my human resource manager. And when we looked at the law, we concluded that indeed, if we were doing a separation of church and state issue, we probably wouldn't come down this way." For Chiounard it was a diversity issue, not a legal issue.

As of the time of my interview Chiounard still thought the question of the law and rulings from the court were irrelevant. But was there really a way for him to say, I'm going to take the diversity perspective and not the *legal* perspective?

"It's a tough one to sell. Yeah, you bet. Because the people keep coming back with, 'The Supreme Court says this.' And I'm saying, 'This is not a Supreme Court issue when it's coming to the aspect of employment law within an employee, within an employment sphere here.'"

It isn't?

"Inside this organization we can say, 'You know what? We don't want Christmas trees. We don't want any religious symbols up.' If somebody might say, 'Well, the Supreme Court says we get to do that,' and we, and we say, 'No, the Supreme Court says that an organization cannot promote that.'"

Chiounard, in fact, is a perfect example of the amateur constitutionalists who occupy positions of power in America—and who make up the law as they go along.

"What we're saying is, 'Due to our efforts at inclusion, and the fact that some people find displays of Christmas stuff offensive, we're gonna say, In our atmosphere we don't want that.' We wanna remain more neutral, for both the public and our employees."

With the wolves baying at his door, Johnson read the Supreme Court decisions and changed the policy, but he refused to cave in during the controversy. He held tough until the New Year, and in early January announced that the policy had been changed back to what it had been before, but asked employees not to offend the feelings of others by putting up trees if there were objections. With that, Christmas trees became unbanned in Eugene.

"I was both, well, I would say I was disappointed," Lauren Chiounard said, looking back on the defeat. "But I understood it. What I felt like what had happened was, the majority spoke out and said, 'How dare you,' and Jim backed down off the issue."

Before Christmas that year, while the controversy was still raging, Johnson had decided to change the policy later, after the bleeding was done. He called in his diversity committees. "I met with the employees that I had met with the first time and said, 'Look, I just, for a variety of reasons, I'm not gonna do this again.' And they all, they were really sorry that I was personally going through all this, that they kind of had caused this hateful speech towards me as an individual. So there are a number of them that said, 'Well, why don't you change it, it's okay, go ahead and change it.' I decided to stick with the policy as written, to ride it out and to change it for future years."

Did any other official ever call Johnson to inquire about instituting a ban on Christmas trees?

"Literally, I had one phone call. It's from a school district in Washington, in the State of Washington, who wanted to know. 'Cause they were being asked to ban Christmas trees and wanted to know the implications of doing that." Johnson laughed when he thought about the call. "So I sort of explained it to 'em, and gave 'em some suggestions on, well, You need to do some more reading, you need to look at some footnotes and small text and some of the Supreme Court decisions."

Chiounard still isn't buying it. He thinks the Christian majority simply bullied Johnson into submission.

"Now Jim will tell you that he backed down due to Supreme

Court decisions or something like that. I don't think there's anybody in the world that could've taken us to court and won that court case against us. Not for, not for what we were doing and the context in which we were doing it."

But the original policy—no ban on Christmas trees—still stands in Eugene?

"It still stands," said Chiounard. "I mean, it's basically, if you wanna have a Christmas decoration, you gotta talk it over with your people in your unit. If somebody objects vehemently to it, it's probably not a good idea. And we'd appreciate it if you wouldn't do that, knowing that that person is probably gonna be very reticent to speak up, because every one of those people in the organization saw what happened."

Chiounard's worst moment in the crisis also came when he was threatened. "So this guy writes in and he says something about, We gotta stop Lauren, 'This dyke bitch.'" Some angry citizens interpreted Chiounard's name as a woman's.

"And, 'I'm gonna come to Eugene and we'll watch his house burn.' We were getting that sort of intensity out of people."

Are they sorry they did it?

"Ya know, I don't think that I am," Jim Johnson said, in the peace of the present day, distant from the turmoil. "It certainly, within the organization and within our community, raised the issue of different religions and different thinking, different thoughts, diversity issues in general were very much in the news. So, if I contributed to a little bit more understanding of the significance of why people think of, that they are personally upset with and harmed by the general population pushing their religion on minorities, if I contributed to them, that's great. It was difficult at the time, but it slowly went away in the January, February months. And then, I knew that I was gonna change it, and there wouldn't be any controversy the next year."

And there was not.

What about Chiounard, the radical anti-Christmas bureaucratic reformer?

"So to me, what that did to me was say, 'We did the right thing,'" Chiounard said, with the typical eagerness in his voice. "To a lot of people, they were saying, 'You did the wrong thing. Look at the response you're getting.' And I'm saying, 'Hell, you know Rosa Parks woulda gotten the same response, you know. Does that mean she was wrong?'"

Rosa Parks, of course, was a devout church woman who might have been shocked to hear her name used to justify banning Christianity and its Christmas trees.

Christmas trees are legal again, but peace has not returned to Eugene. Easter time 2005, the Eugene *Register Guard* was filled with letters to the editor complaining that Christians were putting small signs in their yards, reading HE IS RISEN.

"Can't they keep it to themselves?" readers demanded.

One letter writer complained about people with Christian fish symbols on their cars who were exceeding the speed limit.

The overall message of Easter 2005 from the tolerant liberals of Eugene was that tolerance doesn't extend to Christians.

The Christmas tree ban may return to Eugene yet.

CHAPTER 6

INDIANAPOLIS, INDIANA:

THE LAW SCHOOL EVICTS A TOTALLY LEGAL CHRISTMAS TREE

The Christmas tree battle at Indiana Law School had its beginnings in the suspicions of Christian students that their views, especially on the law, were only tolerated by the faculty, not taken seriously. Leaders of Christian student groups complained to each other that while they were heard out during class, their arguments were given no weight or credence, and in fact were dismissed simply because they were Christian ideas, ideas founded in religion.

Into this wary scenario between conservative Christian students and what they believed was a secularized and entirely liberal faculty entered an out-of-towner. A native Australian, Anthony Tarr was entirely unprepared for the American culture wars he would encounter as dean of the law school. Tarr had visited the United States many times, and was married to an Americanized Australian. But in 2002 he had only just arrived in Indianapolis to begin his first stint as a working resident of the United States when controversy struck.

For Tony Tarr the holidays were a time for fun and lightheartedness, whether it was the Fourth of July or Halloween or Christmas. He especially liked the American proclivity for decorating, and he brought the fervor of the convert to the weekend projects of decorating for the Fourth, or Halloween, or Christmas. For Dean Tarr decorating for holidays had become a method of assimilating into the new American culture that surrounded him.

His wife, Julie-Ann, an Australian who had lived in the United States for fifteen years and knew it much better than her husband, described his mind-set about Christmas this way in an e-mail to me: "Tony came to the U.S. from Australia over three Christmases back." That would make Dean Tarr's first Christmas in America 2002, the Christmas before the great Christmas tree debacle. "This matters for two reasons," Julie-Ann Tarr said. "One, he doesn't carry with him the same sense of perceptual baggage as might those of us who have lived through a lot of formative experiences over the last couple of decades in the U.S. on the freedom of religion, practices, beliefs front." Julie-Ann had spent her fifteen years in the United States attending Cornell and becoming a lawyer. She was keenly aware how different Tony Tarr was going to find Christmas in America from Christmas in Australia. "Two, he is from a place where Christmas comes in the middle of summer, is extremely hot, and doesn't get dark until around ten. That means, in relation to the latter, that there isn't much point in putting up the types of decorations we are talking about around here because you can't see them and it is too hot to care."

Nonetheless, Tony Tarr was aware that the Americans who surrounded him did care, and he decided he should join in. "One of the things Tony couldn't get over when we moved here was the way our city 'decorates,'" Julie-Ann Tarr wrote. "As the 4th of July arrived, hundreds of flags, a mini-parade and assorted oratorical moments unfurled big league on our block." In her e-mail to me, Tarr's wife reported him as slightly startled. "Gee," Julie-

Ann quoted her husband as saying, "They really know all the words to all those songs . . . most Australians fake the lyrics of the national anthem once you get past the first few lines."

Of course, as every American knows, what follows the flags and bunting and fireworks and red, white, and blue plastic plates and cups of the Fourth is the season of three big holidays, the fall. "He then discovered Halloween (and did a mighty fine 15 foot spider web decoration for the yard), Thanksgiving and, finally, the Griswold moment to end all Griswold moments: Christmas." She was, of course, referring to a level of suburban American excess exemplified by Chevy Chase's Griswold family.

As Christmas 2002 approached, the Tarr household prepared for the Christmas break from work and the law school. This time off promised to be great fun: rounds of parties, shopping for gifts, and of course an opportunity for Tony Tarr to indulge his new American self. He could go buy strings of lights, lots and lots of them.

His wife wrote of the process: "After reviewing Chevy Chase's lighting techniques, he disappeared to Lowe's and came home with his 'first set of lights.' Being Australian and naive, it was 50 feet long and, as he attempted to put it on a tree in the backyard, the result made Charlie Brown's Christmas tree look pretty stalwart in comparison. So he went out again (under cover of night) and bought several hundred more yards of lights and set to. And got the front yard, too, this time."

Having festooned the Tarr house with lights on the roof, the chimney, the doors, the windows, the fences, the walkway to the front door, and the front door itself, Tony Tarr was feeling proud of himself, and he went to bed confident that he had more than kept up with the American Joneses. He was wrong.

Julie-Ann Tarr wrote, "As we pulled out of drive the next day, he looked up to find our neighbors had not only just as many lights but also an inflatable seven-foot Santa on their balcony. Another (house) had a cherry picker on their lawn outlining all their trees (in lights), and several others made the North Pole look like amateur land. So he went once more to Lowe's—but this time with that quiet determination that always spells no-good for our bank account. He returned with the makings of what turned out to be a 12 foot kangaroo with a red nose—which ended up on the front of the house." Julie-Ann Tarr was proud of her Americanized Australian husband. "And it looked damn fine. Or so the assorted Christmas-light tour buses said as they came through."

In his first attempt at an American Christmas Tony Tarr had accomplished the difficult chore of wowing Christmas lights tourists as they made the rounds of participating neighborhoods in buses. He was even featured in a local newspaper story about Christmas decorations, and got the concluding quote in the article: "I've learned to never mess with professionals, and you Hoosiers are true professionals when it comes to Christmas lights."

So the next year Tony Tarr was all teed up with Christmas spirit American-style. He expected another great American Christmas season with friends and family, and instead he stepped into the crossfire of Christian students and secular professors.

It was just before Thanksgiving 2003, and Dean Tarr and the office manager of the law school were discussing what to do to decorate the atrium of the main building of the law school for the coming Christmas season. Tarr remembers telling the office manager to put up a tree, but to try to make it an international theme, perhaps with tree ornaments representing all the countries of the world. His hope was that it would turn out to be a secular tree that wouldn't seem to represent any particular religion, but simply be a decoration for the generalized holiday season.

"To be frank, I didn't, when speaking with the office manager, go into the details of decorations," Tony Tarr said, looking back. "We were simply talking about, it would be nice to have this bare atrium looking a little bit more in a holiday festive mood."

Even though the ornaments were internationalized, it didn't work out quite the way he had hoped. "The tree that arrived had a great big star on it, and it had gift parcels below. So I guess it was arguable, in the eyes of people who wanted to see a Christmas tree, that it was, indeed, a Christmas tree," Tarr said.

Julie-Ann Tarr wrote that her husband was not unaware of the constitutional waters that were now sloshing around his chin. "In all fairness, it wasn't without a base understanding of the issues attached to first amendment, the public forum doctrine and the surrounding religious implications. He was certainly aware of the Supreme Court line on trees as non-sectarian, but didn't actually see it as pertinent to his tree. He liked the tree, thought it was a nice symbol of a positive message of good will."

Almost the moment the tree was put up goodwill was the first casualty. Three people objected to the public display of the tree, and they objected on the grounds that it was a symbol of Christianity.

Jon Mayes was president of the Christian Legal Society student chapter that year, and he happened to be sitting in the atrium talking with a friend when the workers suddenly arrived and inexplicably began to take the Christmas tree down. "It was a little odd that they were taking down the Christmas tree several weeks before Christmas. So we asked, 'Why are you taking down the Christmas tree?' And they said, 'Well, somebody complained about it.'"

Mayes sent an e-mail to one of the deans of the law school asking if the issues could be discussed. "She sent me some canned response, basically, not wanting to talk about it," he said to me in an interview. Elizabeth L. DeCoux, assistant dean for student affairs, had said in an e-mail, "The law school is committed to diversity, and because of that commitment, decorations celebrating the New Year and diversity will appear in the atrium in the next few days. I have not seen them, but I believe they will be very festive and will promote good cheer."

On the student-run blog Joshua Claybourn reported an e-mail he had received from the dean for external affairs, Jonna Mac-Dougal. "The tree came down because there were members of the law school community who thought it was divisive and inappropriate. The school will be putting up another holiday decoration to replace it, I think today, if at all possible. There were individuals who believed that the tree sent the wrong message to the law school community and would make some people feel excluded."

At the time Claybourn received this e-mail the identity of the professor who had objected was still not known, though it was suspected. It later turned out that one of the people who had complained about it was Florence Wagman Roisman, a sixty-three-year-old professor of property law, and two students, who were not named. All three were Jewish and had told Dean Anthony Tarr they felt the tree was exclusionary, that it included only Christians in the holiday celebration and left others out.

Florence Wagman Roisman had begun practicing law at the Federal Trade Commission (FTC) in 1963. In 1964, she joined the U.S. Department of Justice in the appellate section of the

Civil Division. In 1967, she became a staff attorney, and later a managing attorney, for the D.C. Neighborhood Legal Services Program (NLSP). That was the start of a thirty-year association with the federally financed program of civil legal assistance to poor people. Her bio emphasizes that while at NLSP she was co-counsel in several of the landlord-tenant cases that now appear in many property casebooks. In 2000, she received the Thurgood Marshall award given by the District of Columbia Bar. In 1989, she was the first recipient of the Kutak-Dodds prize, awarded by the ABA's Standing Committee on Legal Aid and Indigent Defendants and the National Legal Aid and Defender Association.

"She's a very hard-core liberal," Jon Mayes said, "and would just rant and rave. I had her for my first-year property class. And, and, like I said, I have a mutual respect for her because she's very passionate about what she does. But she is a troublemaker in the sense that she is constantly looking for ways, like this Christmas tree, to just prod, you know, How far can I push the liberal agenda?"

(Even Professor Roisman later referred to herself as one of the most liberal faculty members on campus, in a 2005 controversy about tenure for another professor.) Josh Claybourn agreed. "She is a relatively new member of the faculty, pretty highly respected in her field. But she's generally regarded, among students, and I think you could find some faculty to say this off the record, as the most left-wing professor at the school.

"And, it rubs a lot of conservative students the wrong way, of course. But when people found out faculty members were against the Christmas tree, people pretty much guessed it would be her, and their guesses were correct. It turned out to be her."

Professor Roisman has refused to discuss the matter and referred inquiries to her statement, which was issued about two weeks into the raging controversy. "The center of the discussion at the IU School of Law—Indianapolis is not a tree but the question: How do people of different faiths and different philosophies best work, live, and learn together?" she wrote, in a tone that was more hopeful than certain. Perhaps even the professor was surprised by the trouble she had stirred up this time.

"I objected to the official display of the Christmas tree because it is a symbol of one religion, Christianity. I believe that such a display is of doubtful constitutionality in a state-supported law school, but my principal objection is one of policy, not law."

The conservative law students seized on the issue of legality immediately: The Christmas tree was not a violation of the law, and its presence in the atrium of the law school did not run counter to decisions of the United States Supreme Court.

"The Supreme Court in County of Allegheny versus the ACLU said that Christmas trees are steeped in our nation's tradition and aren't considered religious," law student Mayes noted, with barely concealed disgust that the Supreme Court's opinion on the religious status of the tree was so easily ignored. "And the whole thing that the proponents of removing the tree clung to was, 'Well, we're just trying to make sure that diversity is encouraged.' That's because they knew they'd lost the legal argument."

In fact, in her prepared statement Roisman argued the Supreme Court had not declared the Christmas tree a secular symbol, and the only way one could regard the tree was as a religious symbol. She referred to commentary describing the tree as secular by Justice Harry Blackmun as "dictum," and therefore not a "ruling."

"Meaning it wasn't pertinent to the Supreme Court's decision," Mayes said. "They didn't have to decide that issue to decide what was before them in County of Allegheny versus ACLU. While she may be correct, it's Supreme Court dicta, which is pretty powerful." More powerful, say, than the opinion of an obscure law professor in Indiana.

What the Christian students couldn't shake was that it appeared that a perfectly legal Christmas tree was evicted because of someone who admitted that her objections were not based in law and this was, after all, a law school.

To Professor Roisman the issue was Christianity. "My principal objection is that the official display of a symbol of one religion conveys to those of us who subscribe to other religions or philosophies that we are less welcome, less valued, not fully part of the community; that we are allowed to be present by sufferance only. I certainly do not believe that the Christmas tree was erected with the intention of sending that message, and I understand that some non-Christians did not take that message from the display of the tree. But the Christmas tree conveyed that message to me and to others—students, staff, and faculty; and it certainly is not unreasonable for those of us who are not Christians to take that message from the Christmas tree."

Dean Tarr had experienced difficulties with this professor before, and he had decided to ignore her objections. "One of the faculty here who's renowned for taking very strong views on these sort of matters communicated with me. I wasn't motivated by her response to do anything about it," he said to me.

Part of the reason Dean Tarr decided to ignore Professor Roisman, he said, was that she was one of a group of faculty who, in his opinion, had politicized his effort to put a large American flag in the atrium. It was just after the Fourth of July and Tarr thought it odd that the school did not display, in fact did not have, what he thought was a proper flag. But when he decided to put up a flag, framed and mounted with an inscribed plaque noting the historical relevance of the flag, he was deluged with objections from faculty members who accused him of improper political support for a controversial president and a highly divisive war.

But while Tarr had decided to ignore Professor Roisman, at the same time two students had also spoken to him while he was in the atrium to inspect the tree. They were Jewish, and they objected because they thought the tree was just a little too much, too big, too imposing, and asked him, Couldn't he do something that made them feel a little less excluded, or left out? "And I thought about it. And, as I put the decoration there, I thought, 'Well, yeah, I could, actually.'"

Tarr had an idea that would be less Christmas and still Christmasy, if there could be such a thing. Dean Tarr described to the two Jewish students an alternative idea for the atrium holiday decorations, which would be, in his words, "a typical Indiana winter woodlands scene. And I suggested to them that I do something along the lines of what we, in fact, did. And they were happy." This scene would replace the large Christmas tree and would involve at least two evergreen trees, a sleigh, and snow-covered ground.

Dean Tarr was a lawyer, of course, and he was aware that there was the potential for legal issues, but he had thought through the twists and turns of Supreme Court decisions and felt confident he could legally do exactly what he was doing. "The first point, I guess, that is of some significance, is that [the office manager] and I decided to put up a tree. So we weren't taking away someone else's tree." In other words, when he removed the tree he was abridging his own free expression and not someone else's. "When we removed this one tree, we substituted another decoration, which was in the form of two trees and a sleigh. I asked the people who installed this one large tree to substitute an alternate decoration that could be described as, if you had a very natural imagination, an Indiana woodland scene. And, anyway, unfortunately, the company that were responsible for both decorations couldn't achieve the simultaneous changeover. So there was a gap of about thirty-six hours.

"And into that gap plunged all sorts of people with weird and amazing notions of what this represented."

Dean Tarr was referring in part to his own hypervigilant Christian students, who were keenly aware that their personal views on a variety of matters ran counter to the views of the professors who could pass or fail them. The Christian students had learned to conform in the classroom, but only for the purposes of grades and getting through law school. Like many students in college elsewhere, the Christian students here felt that their fate often depended on their ability to ignore their own beliefs and parrot back the views of the professors.

One of the Christian law students wrote in another e-mail that the issue of liberal indoctrination in the classroom was on the minds of many Christian students. "I also brought it up before class with people," the student wrote to one of his friends, also a Christian student, "and they said they usually just pretend to be indoctrinated to get the grade and then go on believing their same values. It seems that a large number of people do think they need to offer a non-Christian view on exams in order to pass."

So the Christian students were in a state of extra watchfulness even before the Christmas tree incident, but when it was taken down they were positive they had caught the school in what they believed was yet another incident that demonstrated an anti-Christian bias.

Claybourn and Mayes weren't alone in their objections. Mayes said, "One other student also e-mailed Dean Tarr. And he sent us both a response that we also copied to the faculty, saying—'I wish to—curtail any further—discussion on the matter. It's closed.' I mean, it wasn't even open to discussion. A rather cold response."

Dean Tarr may have wished to end the matter quickly, but his wishes in the matter were not to be. "And then the other student who sent Dean Tarr an e-mail sent what Dean Tarr told him to the rest of the student body—and it completely blew up," Mayes said. Suddenly the disappearing Christmas tree at Indiana law school had become an issue of enormous passion. "Everybody, whether they were Democrat, Republican, were up in arms over the under-the-table dealing that happened, where one professor and perhaps a couple of students complained about it, and they were the ones that were able to dictate what happened."

Students were outraged because no one could offer a reason under the law that the tree had to be taken down, and after all it was a law school, where the law should come first. "We have an annual lighting of the world's largest Christmas tree. It's actually a monument strung with lights, and in Indianapolis they call it the world's largest Christmas tree," Mayes said in our interview. "And to have, just a few blocks away at the law school, a Christmas tree that is a constitutional breach of the separation of powers, separation of church and state—the absurdity of it. If you go to our state capital in Indianapolis, there is a nice, big Christmas tree inside. That's where the state Supreme Court is."

It wasn't just the Christian students who were upset. The news media picked up the story, and soon the airwaves and newsprint were filled with it.

The BBC ran a story, and in Los Angeles it made drive-time radio news. The Tarrs were getting calls and e-mails from their friends around the world, wondering what was going on. Julie-Ann described the ensuing holiday season onslaught as "hundreds of hate mail messages, letters, phone calls, dinner party meltdowns . . ."

What was supposed to be Tony Tarr's second American Christmas turned into a season in hell.

Julie-Ann described one incident in an e-mail to me: "When we were bailed-up at a friend's house over Christmas drinks, a rather patronizing graduate student from Bloomington's law school (which, incidentally, banned trees nine years ago) in quite small words, *slooowly* explained to Tony that 'here in America— unlike the rest of the world—we embrace diversity. You should not try to stomp it out; you should not be afraid of it. You should embrace it. Put up torahs, put up symbols of other holidays, make the spirits of all live through embracing diversity.'"

This kind of smarminess did not go down well with the Australian. "Tony's response? 'I get it. I get it. What you don't get is that we are a *law* school. Celebrate diversity? We not only celebrate it daily—as lawyers we actually get paid for doing so! I thought it might be kind of novel just for once to find something that we could all feel unifies us.'"

Tony Tarr wasn't prepared for all that came his way. "Well, you should know that we received death threats about this," he said in an interview with me. "Indeed, I arrived home one evening. And my wife, who is absolutely no shrinking violet, was on the telephone. And it transpired that some religious nut from down in

Georgia or somewhere had suggested this notion about her being
married to this Antichrist person." Tony Tarr was a practicing
Episcopalian and at the moment he was being inundated by
e-mail, letters, phone calls, and abuse on the airwaves for a perceived bias against Christians and Christmas trees; his house was
aglow with miles of Christmas lights; and his special twelve-foot
Christmas kangaroo with the red nose was perched on the front
yard. "So anyway, she said, 'Well, wait, wait. Did you know that,
you're quite wrong here.'" The irrepressible Julie-Ann was about
to have a bit of sport with the angry Christian from Georgia who
had managed to find Tony Tarr's home phone number, and the
fun centered around a sixty-five-pound chocolate Santa Tony had
purchased to raffle off at the law school for a charity. "And she
said, 'Did you know that my husband purchased a sixty-five-
pound chocolate Santa and was raising money for an abused child
fund here in Indianapolis through a raffle?' And he said, 'Well,
what the f--- has that got to do with anything?' And that's when
her line came: 'Because if you were here, I'd stick it up your orifice.'"

Tony Tarr still laughs recalling that moment. Nonetheless, he
regretted acceding to the two students' request to remove the tree
almost immediately. "I felt that if, by the simple expedience of
putting another one in place that was less overtly associated with
a religious symbol, I could solve the problem. It seemed like a
good idea at the time," Tarr said to me. "Of course I've, as I told
you, I reflected upon it afterwards, and realized it was a damn stupid idea."

Quickly, he took that back. "Sorry, to qualify that, I mean, I
don't think it was a stupid decision. I think it was more that making the change probably brought more grief than was necessary in
the circumstances. I did not, I guess, appreciate the extent to

which issues going to trees or flags generate this wild emotion that doesn't seem to be grounded in anything."

If the Tarrs are bitter about anything, it was the notion of Tony being anti-Christian. "And certainly you don't want the facts to interfere with the story. It didn't matter whether there might sort have even been a tree inside the building that was originally there, but the fact that someone has reported that some person has taken away a tree brought out all of this venting from a lot of people that were not in the least bit concerned with the facts."

Julie-Ann, as she was packing the family two years later for a move far, far away—a job at the law school in Fiji—said she was left with this memory: "The fact that we still had assorted trees and decorations at our house (and tour buses again) was not registered. Nor was the fact that during final exams lifting spirits with lights, trees—or anything else that sends the message that 'this, too, will pass'—isn't a bad thought."

"With the benefit of hindsight," Tarr said two years after the incident, "I might have said to the two students that approached me, as I understood their point of view, it was not intended in any way to offend any particular religious group, and perhaps next year we might move to having something that was less closely associated, in the minds of viewers, with a particular religion. That's what I may have done."

But the Christian students were left with the feeling that there was more to it than one Australian administrator who had made a mistake in giving in to the heartfelt but nonetheless groundless objections of two students out of hundreds. To the Christian students the whole incident illustrated an anti-Christian bias, an attempt to suppress Christianity.

"Absolutely. You see it across the board," Jon Mayes wrote in an e-mail to me. "I think we've seen it on a national level, in the gay rights arena. The debate is not an attempt to have a public discourse on the matter and resolve it and reach amicable solution. It is, 'We're going to get our way however we can. And without as many people knowing as is possible.'

"And that's why you see the liberal agenda and the gay rights agenda going to the courts. Because it's not publicized as legislation."

But to Mayes, it's even bigger than that. "It's more of a bucking of our entire nation's history of having and holding and celebrating Christmas. And that Christmas tradition is so steeped in our nation's history, that's really what liberals are fighting against, they're fighting that history. They want us to somehow erase our history and traditions and memory of all that, and try and move forward in a completely neutral setting. Well, neutral in the sense that they're just trying to impress one view, the anti-Christian point of view."

The fact that Dean Anthony Tarr intended none of that didn't impress Mayes. The fight was so bitter and so raw that Tarr's ignorance of the battle was no excuse. "I think he still was somewhat of a pushover," said Mayes.

The next year Dean Tarr did not put up any holiday decoration at all in the law school atrium. He also did not put up his miles of Christmas lights at home, and only agreed to bring the twelve-foot kangaroo out of storage when the neighbors almost begged to see it again. And when he did put the kangaroo on the lawn, the light of the red nose had burned out. He couldn't be bothered to screw in a new one.

CHAPTER 7

MAPLEWOOD, NEW JERSEY:

THE HOME OF THE SERIAL CHRISTMAS KILLER

By Christmas 2004, Maplewood, New Jersey, a leafy, upscale bedroom community of New York City, might have become the most famous Christmas battleground in the country.

Within a period of two short years the South Orange/Maplewood School District had issued two radical, eye-popping, and newsmaking anti-Christmas rulings.

In December 2002, an order from the school district offices canceled a grade-school field trip to see a dramatic production of the Dickens classic *A Christmas Carol,* with an explanation to students in classrooms the decision was made for reasons of "religious content." In December 2004, *instrumental* versions of Christmas music were banned in the schools—an expansion of the policy that already banned the lyrics of Christmas carols.

That was a jaw-dropper. What could be so corrosive about "Silent Night" that the school district needed to guard against even the possibility someone might be softly muttering the words "Christ the savior is born" to himself or herself?

What in the world was going on in Maplewood, New Jersey?

The answer: Peter P. Horoschak, the superintendent of schools and a serial Christmas killer.

For the past three decades Horoschak has made his living as a school superintendent, zigzagging across the country from school district to school district as jobs became available. And oddly enough, where Horoschak went a war on Christmas seemed to ensue.

When he was in Shaker Heights, Ohio, twenty-three years ago the school board insisted on a policy that was an almost complete ban on all things Christmas. Four years later, when he was in Albuquerque, New Mexico, a musical director was fired on Horoschak's watch for defying orders not to play Christmas music. Every district Horoschak has worked for has had a restrictive Christmas policy.

Peter Horoschak is sixty-three years old, a tall man with a drooping face and a little white stubble of hair on his head. When I visit him he is dressed in a blue blazer, a button-down shirt and tie, and khaki pants. He has been a school superintendent or assistant to the superintendent for over thirty years. He explains away the disappearance of Christmas in the Maplewood school system as nothing more than a common, mundane matter of curriculum, another of the usual decisions on what to teach the kids.

Plus, he says, there's the issue of how to be fair to non-Christians, whose worship does not conveniently fall in the Christmas season.

"You know, it comes to the holiday time in December, it's mostly Christmas. Hanukah may or may not fall close to it," Horoschak says in the manner of a physician calmly informing you that it's not such a bad thing to have a leg amputated. "It's certainly not the same kind of a holiday for Muslims. Ramadan falls in there, but, you know, how do you celebrate Ramadan? There probably isn't even a tradition of music and all that goes with that. There are other faiths that might feel that they are being left out. And so what's the right mix and how do you do that? Are two-to-one songs the right mix, and you get into those kinds of discussions."

Well, you actually *don't* get into those discussions. Not in the Maplewood school district, anyway. Here the solution to the difficult problem of weighing a little Christmas against a little Hanukah against a little Ramadan has been to bar Christian religious references and discuss other religious references as culture or current events, if at all.

It is a convenient policy: It keeps the people who want to suppress Christmas happy, or it did until 2004, when the controversy became so intense the school board asked Horoschak to revisit the policy and regulation with the objective of quieting the controversy.

Horoschak runs the Maplewood district from an old elementary school building on the edge of the grounds of Columbia High School. Horoschak's office is large, with a personal desk covered in family pictures near a window. Just inside the door is a conference table for twenty where he holds meetings of his staff, or with members of the public, including the occasional parent of a student.

When questioned about his policies he demonstrates lessons hard learned over the years in his insistence that everything done in the school district is at the instruction of the school board. The school superintendent works for the school board. It can hire and fire superintendents. Board members are his bosses.

"This board, this policy has been that, 'look, what we do is, we determine what we teach kids based upon being an approved curriculum by the school board.' The school board approves all curriculum and curriculum changes."

Horoschak and the school board were under enormous pressure because of the international media attention being paid to the ban of instrumental Christmas carols. The original decision to forbid Christmas music came directly from the school board to Horoschak. It had been hyperrational but had demonstrated a tin ear for public sentiment. Unlike past years, this Christmas controversy demonstrated a tendency to stick. The controversy is now getting to the school board.

"Even though the policy may change, because some board members have been elected since and have a little bit different view as to how it should be put in practice," Horoschak says, first offering deference to what might be a change in the thinking of his bosses. "But what we want is . . . we determine ahead of time what we're trying to teach in our music curriculum. And that should then determine what our performances are going to be." I tape recorded an interview with Superintendent Horoschak in his office in the spring of 2005.

In other words, if we're not teaching about Christmas there is no reason to play Christmas music, even if the calendar happens to say it is Christmas week.

Horoschak is setting the curriculum trap for school critics: When someone objects to a policy the administrator often cites the "curriculum." The Maplewood school district immediately took a defensive position behind the curriculum when the national public noticed that even the sound of Christmas was banned in schools in Maplewood, New Jersey.

"And the board wants to look at the issue of concerts around

December and what they should consist of." Horoschak is ready
if the board members ask what other districts do. "You know how
most school districts around here avoid it? They just don't have
concerts in December."

As Christmas approached in December 2004, there was something of a heightened sense of awareness left over from Christmas
2002, when the outing to see Dickens's *A Christmas Carol* was
canceled. Several parents thought that there had been something
exceedingly suspicious about the way the episode had unfolded.

First, the trip was definitely on. The usual form went home
with the students; checks and signatures were required from the
parents. It was entirely a class field trip ordinaire.

Meg Uhlman's daughter, Olivia, was in one of the classes that
was supposed to see the Dickens play. "The permission slip came
home for a team trip—the school is divided into teams—to go
see *A Christmas Carol.* I signed it and returned it," Uhlman said
in an interview with me. Other parents tell the same story: A permission slip came home with the students, along with a request
for a check. The parents signed the form and sent it back with a
check, and a week or two later the students came home reporting
that the trip was off. And the students all reported that the same
reason was given.

Meg Uhlman's daughter Olivia reported that her teacher was
called out of the classroom to see the principal, and when she
came back the teacher said, "Kids, I have some bad news. We're
not going to be going to see *Christmas Carol.* The Board of Ed has
pulled the trip because it has religious content."

Uhlman was incredulous. Religious content? In Charles Dickens's *A Christmas Carol*? What religious content? Ebenezer Scrooge meeting the ghosts of Christmas past, present, and future? Tiny Tim shouting out, "A Merry Christmas to all!" Bob Cratchit wanting Christmas afternoon off to spend a Christmas dinner with his impoverished family and his crippled son?

It didn't make sense, and later the school administrators came up with another reason: Dickens's *A Christmas Carol* was not a part of the curriculum, and the students would not be taking time off from class for a field trip that was not part of the curriculum.

Uhlman spent an hour on the phone with an administrator who insisted it was not a matter of religious content but that it was, in fact, the curriculum issue. Uhlman felt she was being worked by the administrator.

"The teacher told them that," Uhlman said, referring to what her daughter reported. "You can't unring that bell. Those kids were all there. They heard it."

Karen Fabbo also has four children who go to school in the Maplewood district. One of her sons was also part of the canceled trip. "I signed a permission slip, sent in the money. And we were told soon afterwards that the trip had been canceled." But Fabbo did not have any direct contact with the school administration about why the trip was called off. She heard it through her son. "I was told by my son, not by a teacher. And this particular teacher said that it was because of the religious content."

The issue of exactly what religious content was never resolved, but the school district had immediately changed the rationale for the cancellation. For more than a few Christian parents, though, the incident began to conjure up the ghosts of other quasi-religious issues from the past. For Karen Fabbo it was the year her son Anton was in the fifth grade and he was given an assignment to make a poster that demonstrated the concept of diversity.

"His inclination was to put black kids and white kids," Fabbo said, recalling an incident two years back. "And I explained to him that diversity just meant differences. It didn't mean necessarily just black and white. It meant male and female, old and young, and blah, blah, blah, religious differences and all that."

Maplewood is a leafy and privileged community. Neighboring communities are racially diverse, but in Maplewood the diversity is mostly religious: high concentrations of both Jewish and Christian families. It is a state of equilibrium completely out of step with the nation as a whole, in which Christians vastly outnumber Jews, and Muslims, and every other religious sect. "So he proceeded to take pictures from the Internet and paste them on a page. And he was using some religious symbols, the Star of David, I think there was a Muslim one, whatever. And I said, 'You know you could use a Christian symbol as well.' And he said, 'No, I don't want to offend anyone.'" Fabbo related the story in a recorded interview with me.

Fabbo was shocked—but not. Christianity offends someone? "He never got that at home. That's the climate in this town. We're told that all the time."

Fabbo's family is in the South Orange part of the South Orange/Maplewood School District. "I live in South Orange for a reason. I like the diversity. I think it's important for children to have these experiences. And I've always been grateful for the teachers, other parents, and their friends who've been able to let them share with them their cultural or religious backgrounds." But in the five years it took her son Anton to progress from kindergarten to fifth grade, Fabbo said the issue of something being offensive to someone became worse and worse. "Every year it would come up about Halloween. That offended—that could offend—people. Valentine's Day—because it had a *Saint* Valentine connotation. That could offend people. And I was like, 'Where is this going?'

"By the time he got to fifth grade and this instance had occurred, I was really upset. And I said to him, 'You know there's nothing in Christianity that's offensive to anyone.'"

After the Dickens incident Fabbo said the accumulated concern about who was offended and why compelled her to go speak to both the school superintendent and a local rabbi. Neither conversation was satisfactory. Horoschak, it seemed to her, brushed her off, and the rabbi said he was unaware of who could be offended by ordinary things that were connected to Christianity.

But there was more. It started coming back to Fabbo as she reviewed the Dickens incident in her thoughts. "When you're a class parent it's your responsibility to bring in cookies and snacks for certain holiday parties. And in December it's Hanukah and Christmas that we're celebrating. But we were told, 'Make sure that the plates are white or that the plates only have snowflakes on them.' No Christmas trees, no candy canes, no any of that. I remember one year going in and bringing in Hanukah gelt and candy canes for the children. I thought, This is just ridiculous that they're even asking me not to do this. And I kinda did it anyway."

The Fabbo and Uhlman families, both Christian, have the feeling that an anti-Christian air has crept into the town, and they don't know whether to blame the Jewish families who seem to resent Christian or Christmas symbols on display, or other Christian families, who seem to have taken the attitude that their fellow Christians are too numerous, too overbearing culturally, and that the solution is for Christians to take a back seat for a while.

Fabbo stewed over the situation. "There's no word that we have that says you're anti-Christian. You know you can be called a racist. You can be called an anti-Semite. Those words all have power. There's no word that we use that has power about what this is." Then came the Christmas music policy, in which the school district banned the playing of all Christmas carols, even instrumental versions. Superintendent Horoschak said, and we have already seen, that it was nothing new but simply a reiteration of an old policy against the performance of religious music by school choirs, or orchestras, or bands, but it had come to the attention of administrators that instrumental groups had continued to play music that was forbidden and had escaped attention because words were not sung. Now the policy, in place for many years, was being extended to those instrumental bands.

Horoschak's reason, which probably sounded good in the boardroom, didn't wash in the media. Newspapers and news magazines picked up the story, conservative blogs jumped in with a vengeance, and talk radio set the airwaves on fire with outrage. The story caught the attention of the Thomas More Law Center in Ann Arbor, Michigan. Eventually, a school music director at a separate school decided to make a federal case of it and obtained the services of Thomas More Law Center attorney Robert Muise. Muise filed suit in federal court, claiming religious viewpoint discrimination on the part of the South Orange/Maplewood School District.

Horoschak rejected the idea that the school should observe a religious holiday in any way, however small, however inconsequential, however slight. He told me in our interview, "I think that argument makes a point that somehow or other the public school system has a responsibility to reenforce a person's religious views by having participation in the schools of parts of that faith tradition. I would say the question really has to be, What is the role of public education and what should we be teaching children and how should we go about teaching children? And our policies are such that our teaching will not, *will not* promote nor inhibit any particular religious faith, thinking, and practice.

"So, from my point of view, I'm Christian, my family celebrates Christmas, I'm perfectly fine if I look at it as a parent with my children and now my grandchildren learning about their faith and their churches and their home and to have those family celebrations. They don't have to participate in that in school for them to be a part of that."

As for canceling Dickens, Horoschak deflected any charge that it was for religious reasons. "Part of that issue, too, was, believe it or not, there is an attempt to try to have teachers recognize that you ought not to be pulling children out of classroom time for instruction to go to other events unless it's really directly connected to what is being taught and it's going to somehow, you know, elevate the instruction.

"Going off to something just for entertainment or because this time of year they like to do it really uses up some very precious class time, and very often not only the teachers in that subject area, but other subject areas as well. So, in this case it wasn't part of the curriculum."

Peter P. Horoschak was graduated from West Point, class of 1962. He served as commander of a tank unit in Vietnam and returned home to attend Boston College, where he earned a master's degree in education before going on to Harvard, where he earned a doctorate in education.

At age thirty-two, with a young and burgeoning family, Horoschak became the assistant to the superintendent of Boston's schools, William O'Leary. They had been classmates at Harvard and, in fact, Horoschak's doctoral dissertation is a detailed self-study of his tenure working for O'Leary. The dissertation shows a young man who was highly organized, very energetic, and from his army days accustomed to giving orders and seeing to it that they were followed. It was also a tense period in the Boston public schools: A federal judge had just imposed a desegregation order that was extremely controversial, highly divisive, and extremely difficult to carry out.

Horoschak is a very self-confident man and quite capable of handling a problem and a crisis at once. During our conversation, despite keeping a wary eye on his questioner, he is interrupted frequently by insistent staff members who are certain they need his attention—and a fire in a bathroom at the high school. A student has set a bathroom trash can on fire and the school must be evacuated and the smoke blown out before students can return to class. He handles problems efficiently, with a calm demeanor. He is accustomed to command.

He also has some explaining to do. Why do Christmas controversies follow Peter P. Horoschak all across the country? Why do news headlines about yet another outrageous decision banning some aspect of Christmas frequently seem to lead back to a superintendent with the same name: Peter P. Horoschak? His answer to that question is always the same: I implement board policy. The board sets a policy, I carry it out. It is left to coincidence, in his mind, that his career seems to be festooned with more anti-

Christmas policies than that of other men and women in the same job. He deflects any suggestion that Peter P. Horoschak is a serial Christmas killer with a wave of the hand, and a curt response: "board policy." In a subsequent interview, he elaborated: "I have been attracted to communities where issues related to equal opportunity are important."

Let's start at the beginning. How does a military officer trained at West Point end up in a lifelong career as a school superintendent?

"That's not such a stretch, I think," Horoschak says in a soft but firm voice. "When you think about the fact that military service, particularly as an officer, and particularly an officer in combat arms, is a lot of training. It is education. It's working with people and training them to do the job and helping them to aspire to be very good at what they do and be motivating what they do."

When Horoschak was graduated from West Point in 1962 the civil rights era was still in progress, John Kennedy was president, Vietnam was lurking over the horizon, and the legacy of segregated schools and neighborhoods was still very much a reality in American life. Diversity was still a dream.

Horoschak's basic philosophies of education were formed at the service academy. "At West Point, at all the service academies, there's a great deal of emphasis on character development. And much of the things related to these policies deal with people's moral development, character development, and how you create a community that's appropriate for all."

When Horoschak was a cadet at West Point religion was a fixture of life for him and all his classmates. "The days that I went to the service academy, Sunday morning we formed up and marched to chapel. We had a choice of going to one of three religious chapels, and the Jewish kids, the Catholics, and the Protestants marched, and they attended chapel." For someone who has worked so hard to remove all remnants of required religious observation from schools, Horoschak betrays no rancor in his voice. "That changed because of changes in the law and all."

Rumors about Horoschak around Maplewood, especially from those Christian families which view him with suspicion, identify him as Jewish. He is not. "I came from a pretty extensive religious background. My parents are Eastern Orthodox, and I'd gone to church all my life. And so I found attending chapel to be positive because, especially your first year, there was a chance when you could relax and reflect." Prayer time was a chance to escape the not always welcome attention of upper classmen.

A West Point Christmas for young Peter Paul Horoschak was classic 1962 through and through. "Christmas at West Point was only for one year, your first year in those days. You stayed at West Point as a plebe. The upper classes are gone. They went home or wherever they wanted to go, if they got to leave. And so, after your plebe year, then you could leave, and I always went home to my family."

If you stayed at the academy over the Christmas holiday, Christmas was observed in full. "It was a religious holiday; you attended chapel. You were supposed to attend. I'm not quite sure if that was mandated or not." Sometimes officers and their families invited a plebe in for Christmas dinner, or a Christmas party. "When I was there the first year my family came back, and my parents spent time with me during that period."

If there were Christmas traumas at West Point during the formative years of young cadet Peter Horoschak, they appear long buried. He insists his actions as a Christmas cop are simply a matter of following orders, just as he learned to do at West Point. "I don't set policy. I have to see to it that the policy is followed. The Board of Education sets the policy. In every case: Shaker Heights, Albuquerque, here, the policies were in place. And they have been in place."

Before Horoschak arrived for the job in Shaker Heights, Ohio, in 1982, the community had been convulsed by a Christmas controversy. "Shaker Heights, as a matter of fact, had gone through a major, major community . . . I'd like to say it was a dialogue, but I understood it to be a quite contentious time trying to set their policy, what to do about all this.

"In Shaker Heights the policy was that during December you weren't supposed to use even red and green paper; everything was supposed to stay neutral. So that was their policy, and I was superintendent. And of course it's my job to see to it that it's carried out. Now, Shaker Heights was pretty easy to understand. They had already just been through it all, and they knew what they wanted to do and how they wanted to do it.

"They wanted to be very neutral during that period of time in terms of any kind of demonstration of the religious holiday, be it in decorations or be it in performances. All these policies allow for the teaching about religion in the schools and the role that religion plays in the culture and the role religion has played in history."

Horoschak has been away from Shaker Heights for more than two decades, but he sees Maplewood as a very similar place. "The makeup of the groups, racially, religious, national ethnic identity. Very similar. So the fact that the policies would be similar is not unusual. Shaker Heights really did decide that they had to be very firm because you just couldn't satisfy all interests. When you're in a very diverse community, trying to satisfy all interests on matters of culture, it becomes even harder than elsewhere, because sometimes the emotional issues are involved." It was in these formative years in Shaker Heights, Ohio, apparently that Horoschak developed the attitude that a superintendent couldn't make everybody happy about the Christmas holidays, and it was better to simply keep it all out of the schools.

Now in Maplewood, twenty-three years down the road, he has found other reasons that conveniently fit an approach he wants to follow anyway. Christmas is the season of too much: Christmas is in the malls, on the streets, in the media. "I think one aspect of Christmas especially that is of concern to people that do not celebrate it is that their children are inundated with the whole Christmas season and all that goes on with it, and because of all the advertising, all this demand placed on families."

In Horoschak's world kids need to be insulated, protected from Christmas. Christmas is huge, it is overbearing, and some of his parents can't cope with the seasonal invasion of their homes and their kids' lives. "A lot of it is commercial and kids can't get away from it." Parents are on the spot. "They have their children ask questions about it. They have issues that it's overwhelming, and for many people and their families, even some Christian people feel this way."

Christians say Christmas is too much? "That at least at school they ought to be able to get away from that influence for a while, not to be a part of your school environment. I'm not saying that the majority of Christians feel that way, but certainly I've run into those as well. Some people have different levels of toleration of dealing with matters related to other people's religions and how

you go about doing it. So, setting policy in this area is demanding, and it is a board view. Yes, as a superintendent, I'm able to
advise and I'm able to suggest how things might be done. I don't
vote on it. But they expect me to carry it out."

Does Horoschak understand that some parents think a draconian policy that demands not even instrumental Christmas
music be played can be construed not as merely a wall between
Christmas and the people who don't celebrate it, but as something more, something like *hostility* to Christmas and Christians?

"That issue came up after several years of it going on here, particularly one of our instrumental groups. It was a brass ensemble,
and they'd perform in different ways; that got to a lot of different
people. For example, in the hallways of the building during the
holiday time, out at an event in the community, or we even had
them come over here. The staff in this building has a little lunch-
eon, and they'd come over here and they'd play. So, it'd been going on for some time and I didn't object to it under the policy.
Personally, I thought that was fine."

The superintendent's sensibilities in these matters seem finely
attuned. Why was his judgment not good enough?

"However, not only that group, but there were some of the instrumental groups in the schools, secondary level, which were
playing programs that had a lot of Christmas music in them, carols and all. It was just the music. And it came to the board members' attention that this was not part of the policy."

It may have seemed petty to some, but not to the Board of Education.

"I mean, it was in violation of the policy and the board wanted
me to look into it." In fact, the board demanded he crack down
on specific instructions to do so in his annual review. "So, I

looked into it. And I put together a process working with the music teachers about it, which included our director of fine arts, who has the music program as part of his responsibility to the music teachers. We have an in-house attorney who also met and talked with the teachers."

Horoschak wants to avoid religion altogether. "Where I think we need to be putting our time and energy in public schools is in character development, teaching about respect, responsibility, trustworthiness, fairness, caring, civility, being part of a community. And if you are teaching those things and those are being instilled in young people and it's modeled by the adults, then they come to understand about tolerance for other people's faith, the importance of their own community, and how you don't have to practice the faith, the traditions of the faith in the school."

Horoschak is opposed to bringing any of it on the school grounds. If you want your child to be exposed to anything that even seems connected to religion, and Christmas would be one, do it at home.

"We have a major role in helping young people grow up to be very responsible citizens. And that's the reason why, in communities like this one, communities like Shaker Heights, larger cities, you know, for me it was Albuquerque, or Boston where I worked, where there's very diverse populations, it's important to get this right."

Horoschak's approach to religious differences and conflicts was formed by his experience developing an approach to racial differences and conflicts. "It's important to make the distinction between what is truly teaching, developing good character and teaching about those values and, therefore, expecting that these young people as they continue this system and go on to life, will know and understand the values of people having their faith and the practice of their faith protected and involvement and tolerance, and in many cases enjoyment for it. So, I don't even think it should be an issue here."

What's more, Horoschak is suspicious of people who think their Christmas carols have a place in the schools. The people who want that out are not the problem; rather, it's the people who want it in. "I think people that want to come to a school district and push their views and ideas about what ought to be taught or what ought to be promoted in the schools, that has something to do with their own philosophy, their own views, their own faith, their own religion, at the expense of something else, is not right either.

"And I think a lot of people that argue for this have some kind of an idea, that again goes back to the idea that, well, it could be extreme like, well, 'This was a Christian nation. Therefore, we oughta make sure everybody knows and understands that.'"

To Horoschak that idea is anathema because, while it may be true in the nation at large, it can also be definitively not true in the microdemographics of a school district.

"You have very sizable Jewish population here as well as Christian population. And then you have smaller groups of other religious faiths, Muslim, primarily it is those three, the top three, but then there's other smaller groups.

"The idea of teaching about what religion is and the contributions it's made and how people go about doing it and all that, of course, that's part of a curriculum. And that's what the importance of a curriculum happens to be in terms of, Well, what are we going to teach here? We have to make sure we know and understand its place in our culture and the role it plays. And the important role it plays."

But the fact is Maplewood schools' policy is permissive but the regulations implementing the policy are not. The policy says religion is to be taught, but Horoschak believes the Christmas season is not the time.

Horoschak acknowledges he is a key figure in developing policies that the school board adopts, and that his ideas inform the debate among the board members.

"There's a side that says, 'Anything that has to do with religious training or development really ought to be in your own faith community and not in the schools.' There's others that argue, and it's not an argument that I think is wrong, 'we ought to be doing things to demonstrate and to let everybody enjoy each other's culture, to include their religious culture.'"

Good so far. General philosophy inclusive of all.

But then comes the slippery part.

"And that's where it gets to be a matter of policy. The districts that I've worked in that have said that—Shaker Heights and here are probably a little bit stricter in terms of the policies than anywhere else—have said that 'you can't find equilibrium in doing that.'"

In other words, even though many believe the right thing to do is tell kids about the observances of all religions, as a pratical matter it is believed to be impossible, so the best thing to do is say nothing about any religious day whatsoever.

"It's just the idea of satisfying sometimes competing demands. How are we going to be fair and equitable?" Nonetheless, Horoschak thinks the lawsuit and the storm of protest has had an effect. "I think that there's a number of members of this board that would like to see it handled differently."

I asked him in a later interview if he thought the board had put him in a difficult position by demanding he crack down and then later ordering him to find a new solution that would tamp down the controversy that ensued.

"That's the job." He laughed.

While he might be enforcing a different policy in the future, it is clear what Horoschak thinks is a good idea and what is not, and he is clearly dumbfounded that parents want the schools telling the kids about religion at all. That's the job of the parents and the church, in his view.

"We all have our respective roles. Families have a role, schools have a role and also, you know, other social institutions, [including] faith organizations. I mean, there's a lot of other issues that come up about, you know, what the school should be doing about, that are controversial outside of school."

To the Christian lawyer the great annoyance in cases of religious rights is the so-called offended observer, the one minor religionist who complains of being offended at the sight of, or being in the presence of, symbols of the Christian religion such as Christmas and the various tokens of Christmas commonly on display during December.

Horoschak has an entirely different take on the offended observer.

"From time to time someone might be offended, like the Dickens, going to see that. People were offended, apparently, because they felt that their kids should have the opportunity to do that. And, actually, if their kid should have the opportunity to do that, they could make sure they get to do it as well. I took the same position: to go off and see some movie, take elementary school kids off to see some movie around the holiday time, that some teachers thought [that] would be really nice because it's a nice movie. But why are we taking our kids out of school to go see a movie that their parents could take 'em to?"

I told Horoschak of a comment that a lawyer had made to me about the role of a school superintendent: to keep the peace. Most superintendents, this lawyer had confided, will jump when the ACLU calls, and jump again when the Christian lawyers call, because they just try to find a way to operate that nobody objects to. The superintendent wants quiet, peace. Horoschak shakes his head no. He doesn't mind turmoil. He's not in the job with the goal of placidity.

"I'm here for a different reason. Because I have a personal commitment family-wise, as well as personally, as well as what my experiences that took me—in the military and off to war, is that I'm very interested in being part of a society where people of all different backgrounds not only learn to live and appreciate and grow together, but where children of all backgrounds can do very well."

Horoschak's family includes two adopted sons who are African American, who have both married caucasian women, and have interracial children. In addition, one of Horoschak's adult children has adopted an Asian baby.

"I'm very committed to what American education is trying to accomplish on behalf of all kids. And this is the place to do it. But this is the hardest place to do it, when you're trying to figure out what are the issues related to appropriate types of schooling.

"You know, the things that I've dealt with, like starting in Boston, was desegregation. The court imposed desegregation to break up a system that was unfair to a lot of people. And I've been in that sort of situation almost all through my career. And I've chosen that, and maybe have gained some insights about how this sort of thing might best be done. And maybe I've been hired for that."

Doesn't Horoschak see that his rigid anti-Christmas policies can be felt by parents and children as anti-Christian, as policies which are hostile to their relgion?

"I will tell you in my case, and I think a lot of my colleagues, if a board was to develop a policy that was based upon being hostile to religion, I would speak out. I'd speak out to the board. I would speak out to the community about my views. There's plenty of time in the development of that sort of thing where you have a chance to impact it. And, you know, if ultimately as a superintendent, if you get to the point where you feel you cannot carry out the policies of the board because you don't think they're correct, then you need to separate yourself from it.

"Some things have to be worried about, whether or not they're defensible. And, actually, attorneys look over most of these policies. And I think it is important. Because you don't wanna have a policy on religion in the schools that is in conflict with constitutional law or state law. And if you want to make it more strict than what is generally there, in terms of practice, you can do that."

You can see that Horoschak and his colleagues believe the Supreme Court decisions on Christmas are a floor, not a ceiling. He thinks he is perfectly justified in being more restrictive than the Supreme Court says is required. He believes boards can impose more confining rules than the courts recommend and they will be safe.

"And, if the board would choose to say, 'Well, because we're a diverse community and we think that during these periods of time when there's religious observances going on, there's holidays and everything, we ought to try to do more to teach about the culture or perform or something like that and make it somehow representative of the various groups,' then we'd have to figure out how to do that. So, we'll see where it goes."

Would he preside over schools that put up Christmas trees? No, but in Maplewood it is almost irrelevant. "You know, it really depends on the place. Because here you wouldn't find a Christmas tree up in the schools. You know, there just hasn't been one. I think there's an understanding and discussion that they're not going to do that."

Horoschak ought to be nearing retirement age, but he won't be stepping down. For one thing, he says, he's moved around too much to have a proper retirement waiting for him at age sixty-five. Second, he wants to stay on the job and keep holding the courts at bay while he carries out the wishes of his local community.

"In terms of being able to deal with these questions that we're dealing with today, I think the federal courts have a role and they've defined the law. As you said, generally it's whether it prohibits or doesn't prohibit something." Once again, Horoschak turns away from guidance from the court. "Then it ought to be at the local level. They decide what's right for them and their community. And what do we want to do about it? And when it comes to these sorts of cultural issues, in terms of teaching about what values people should have, one of the values is respect for religion and people's religious faith and the importance it plays not only in our country but, I think, in our lives and the benefit that that has."

Christmas is Christian and Christianity is religion and religion is out.

"You should not try to discard it, you certainly shouldn't be hostile to it. But, you know, what suits a community culturally is something that community can figure out. As long as it doesn't violate the law. And I've been comfortable with the types of policies I've had to work with. Even though I've found that in some cases they're hard to implement without having some controversy come up."

Come Christmastime Peter Horoschak usually has a controversy come up. He seems comfortable with his fight to hold the line.

If it were up to him "Silent Night" would still be out.

CHAPTER 8

ONWARD, CHRISTIAN LAWYERS:

THE GUYS WEARING THE WHITE HATS

Nothing happens in America unless it happens in court. No victory is a true victory until it is won in court, and no victory can claim the protection of decided law until it has made its way from state courts to the federal district courts, through the federal appellate courts, and finally through the Supreme Court of the United States.

Therefore, the battles over Christmas have often been lost in the school administrator's office, or the city manager's office, but they have never truly been won until the courts decide the issue. Consequently, in the modern holy wars, it is the crusading lawyer rather than the crusading knight who has carried the burden of the battle.

And the latest phenomena in the war on Christmas is the rise of the Christian lawyer. For many years the ACLU and its secularist cohorts had the run of the courts and were able to threaten and intimidate school administrators and municipal managers into suppressing Christmas with virtually no opposition. The equation seems to have gone like this: Christmas is Christian, and since Christianity is banned, therefore Christmas must be banned also.

Starting with one or two Christian lawyers who felt the ACLU must be challenged, there has been an explosion in public interest law firms that deal exclusively with matters of religion in the public square, and which have been called into action annually as regularly as the calendar turns from October to November to December.

So who are these lawyers who have forsaken lucrative practices to fight for religious rights? Here are descriptions and some of the thoughts of the most prominent of the new breed of Christian lawyers whose names are behind the most important fights of the Christmas season. I conducted recorded interviews with each in the spring of 2005.

JOHN WHITEHEAD, THE RUTHERFORD INSTITUTE, CHARLOTTESVILLE, VIRGINIA

John Whitehead is fifty-nine years old, a lawyer educated at the University of Arkansas who turned to cases involving religious rights in 1982 when he took up the defense of a Christian church in the San Francisco Bay Area that was being sued by a gay organist who admitted later he had maneuvered to get himself hired, declared himself gay, and sued after he was dismissed by the church. Whitehead won that case, establishing the right of a church to hire on the basis of adherence to faith doctrines.

"I just started seeing the Christmas cases about [the] early nineties," said Whitehead. "But really, if you look back, there's constant parallel streams working here. One is what's been taught in the public schools since the sixties or early seventies, this idea that anything religious, especially Christian, is unconstitutional. It's suspect and should be eliminated. It's taken about thirty years to foment, but it's here now." Whitehead spoke to me in a recorded interview conducted in the spring of 2005.

"It's in the workplace. You have these corporations now saying that you can't have Christmas trees, you can't have Santa Claus. I had a guy who called me and talked about the Christmas party, actually a holiday party now, and he said people would *whisper* Merry Christmas in each other's ears. So Christmas and Christianity have become politically incorrect over a period of time.

"At the same time, though, religious belief has strengthened in this country. Where Christians at one time just kind of wanted to fit in, many of them don't anymore. They want to do their job. They want to be able to go to school and do things. But they don't want their faith demeaned, and they won't take a back seat.

"A case that we worked on during Christmas, I think it was the state of Washington. A woman had a kid in elementary school, and mothers could bring in cookies and stuff during the holidays. Well, right before Christmas she was going to bring in a cake that said 'Happy Birthday Jesus' on it. She's coming down the hall with the cake, and the principal sees her, and says, 'What is this?' And she opens it up and they see that Jesus name on there. And they say she can't go in the classroom with it.

"The courts have said that if you have different viewpoints, you cannot discriminate against the religious viewpoint. That's what trumps in the cases like the mother with the Christmas cake. You can't allow someone with 'Happy Holidays' or whatever, and then throw out 'Happy Birthday Jesus.'

"The nativity scene bans that we've seen over the years really come from those 1960s court cases where courts said prayer, Bible reading, those kind of things were outlawed in schools. But some courts took it too far. The ACLU does some good things, but they have a really bad blind spot when it comes to religion. The ACLU and another group, Americans United for Separation of Church and State, foment this idea that anything religious is unconstitutional.

"Schools routinely have the menorahs during Christmas. They have Kwanzaa. They sing Jewish Hanukah songs, and they show kids the dreidel toy, but then someone comes in and says, 'Let's have a Christmas tree,' and they go bonkers. In my opinion, what we've seen over the last ten years is a decidedly anti-Christian bias.

"The argument used was 'tolerance and diversity.' So it's a classic example where political correctness becomes intolerance in the name of tolerance. And it's a little scary.

"Hopefully, they'll get it over a period of time. But I just hope it hasn't gone too far. I mean, now there's just an outright prejudice. And I don't know how you reverse prejudice like that.

"Christians have gotten to the point where they say, We're not going to take it any more. Enough's enough. We're going to go into the workplace. We're going to go in the schools, and we're going to practice our religion like everybody else does theirs. And that's why you're seeing the conflict."

JAY SEKULOW, AMERICAN CENTER FOR LAW AND JUSTICE, WASHINGTON, D.C.

The American Center for Law and Justice was founded by Pat Robertson, the evangelist, in 1990 with the expressed purpose of meeting the ACLU on the religious field of battle, the federal courts. Chief counsel Jay Sekulow is forty-nine years old, a Jew who converted to Christianity, and is credited, even by his opponents, as one of the most able and persuasive lawyers practicing in the area of religious freedom.

People for the American Way, a liberal advocacy group, credits Sekulow with two landmark Supreme Court decisions: In *Board of Education of Westside Community Schools* v. *Mergens,* Sekulow argued for the right of public school students to form Bible clubs and religious organizations on their school campuses. In *Lamb's Chapel* v. *Center Moriches School District,* Sekulow defended the rights of religious groups to use public school property for religious meetings after hours. Liberal groups also attack Sekulow for his work writing the Defense of Marriage Act, which was signed into law by President Bill Clinton.

"What has happened over about a twenty-year period," said Sekulow, "is the ACLU had convinced just about every municipality in the country that any type of religious expression, if it was taking place on public property, was unconstitutional. So, we had a lot of educating to do. But then we had, really in the last couple of years, these outrageous decisions [from schools and municipal managers] involving the Christmas tree, and even calling something the Christmas holiday. So there has been an increased secularism, and you couple that with the ACLU on a national campaign on eradicating all the Ten Commandment displays, and you have an orchestrated process of removing anything that had a religious symbolism out of the public square.

"A lot of these school districts are so easily intimidated by a threat of a lawsuit, which can mean an award of attorney's fees, which they would have to pay, so they overprotect. They overdo it. And a lot of what we've had to do is create a tension point. What I mean by that is, the ACLU will threaten a lawsuit and we have to come back around and say, 'Well, if you remove this activity, *we're* going to file a lawsuit.' And what that tends to do is bring a little more balance to it so they're not quite as quick to pull the trigger."

Which of the following are permissible for school officials or municipal authorities to allow on public property:

Christmas carols?

"Fine."

Christmas wreaths?

"No problem. The Christmas tree and wreaths have to be in a setting where there's other symbols represented."

Can they be *called* Christmas trees? "Yeah, yeah. No problem."

Do they have to be called "friendship trees" or "giving trees"? "No."

The Christmas tree itself? "They're fine, but you've got have other things around them. We call it 'the reindeer rule.' You have to have other secular symbols or you have to include other faith symbols. If I was advising the school board, I'd say, 'Do both.'"

What do you say about a school that has scrubbed out even the colors red and green? "Overreaction and ridiculous."

"Christmas" the word? "That's the great dilemma. The word, of course, has a religious connotation. It's an official federal holiday, but it has a clearly religious connotation. I think the Supreme Court, in light of the Pledge of Allegiance language from Justice O'Connor, would probably say it's fine. Although, it's hard to argue that Christmas has lost its meaning, but that's what they would probably say. What they'd probably say is, it's taken on a secular meaning."

RICHARD THOMPSON, FOUNDER,
THOMAS MORE LAW CENTER,
ANN ARBOR, MICHIGAN

Sixty-eight-year-old Richard Thompson is best known as the Oakland County, Michigan, district attorney who prosecuted Dr. Jack Kevorkian and won a conviction on a second-degree murder charge in April 1999.

Thompson founded the Thomas More Law Center on a grant of seed money from millionaire Tom Monaghan, owner of Domino's Pizza and the Detroit Tigers baseball franchise, and founder of the Ave Maria Catholic law school in Ann Arbor, Michigan.

The Thomas More Law Center focuses on religious freedom issues. It has taken on the case of a parent who objected to the banning of instrumental versions of Christmas carols in the Maplewood, New Jersey, school district, and it has sued on behalf of a parent in New York City who objected to a school district policy that bans the crèche or nativity scene from New York City schools.

"The Thomas More Law Center was started in 1999," said Thompson, "when I suggested to Mr. Tom Monaghan, who is a philanthropist and also a very deeply religious person, that the battleground in the cultural war right now is in the courts.

"I told him that the courts have become the dominant institution in our society, virtually having veto power over anything that our elected representatives do. Certain groups, including the ACLU, have free reign in the court system and would be able to change the direction and culture of the country merely by filing lawsuits and being able to convince relatively few people what the law is. I'm talking about judges. And then a particular judge will issue an opinion that will ultimately traverse the entire nation and become the law of the land.

"It was important that people of faith be able to confront the ACLU and other groups, such as Americans United for Separation of Church and State, where the major decisions were being made, and that was in the courtroom. He agreed with me and provided the seed money to get the Thomas More Law Center started.

"Our mission is to promote and defend the religious freedom of Christians, traditional family values, and the sanctity of human life.

"Our concern is that there's been a really insidious agenda out there, primarily prompted by the ACLU, to remove every vestige of Christian symbols from public life. And you know nothing escapes their view, whether it's a cross or a nativity, or a Ten Commandments monument—they're going to take them down. And there's a reason for that. It's out of sight, out of mind. If they can remove all these vestiges of Christianity from the public square, and remove them from the sight of our children, then ultimately it's removing the principles that those symbols stand for. The ACLU started in the 1920s. Their agenda has been a very left-wing liberal agenda, and it has never changed. Basically it is deconstructing the principles of the founding of our nation.

"The establishment clause was never meant to prohibit religious displays or the influence of religion on government. It was really to prevent government's intrusion into religion. And the ACLU has been able to take that clause, turn it on its head, and now use it as a means of removing every vestige of religion from the public square. That's what we're fighting against. Because I believe that the foundations of our nation are Christian principles, and that once you destroy those Christian principles you basically destroy the culture.

"The cultural elite of our society is antireligious, anti-Christian, and they control the mode of expression of most people. And so they are able to push the politicians around, push the school systems around, despite the fact that the parents of the students and the vast majority of Americans consider themselves Christian.

"Christ turned over the tables in the temple. He was not some mealymouthed person. He spoke the truth regardless of whether people believed him or not."

ROBERT MUISE, THOMAS MORE LAW CENTER, ANN ARBOR, MICHIGAN

Forty-year-old Robert Muise is an associate counsel for the Thomas More Law Center, meaning he is frequently one of the lawyers actually litigating religious freedom cases. He grew up in Massachusetts, graduated from Holy Cross University, and went to law school at Notre Dame. Between Holy Cross and law school he spent thirteen years as a Marine Corps officer, fought in the first Gulf War as an infantry company executive officer, and during that time, he said, "I got more concerned about what was happening here culturally."

Muise went to law school specifically to go into the type of law he now practices, religious freedom law. He and his wife have nine children, are devout Catholics, and homeschool their children.

"You know, we celebrate Christmas as a nation," said Muise. "It's a Christian holiday. We should all be promoting education, but it's not forcing people to be Christians. Take our client Miss

Skoros in New York City. Her kid's learning about Hanukah, and what the Jewish menorah means. That is the miracle of the oil. That's wonderful. But why ban the Christian religious symbol, the crèche?

"Liberals claim to be the tolerant ones. But look what they're doing: Christianity has crosshairs on it, and it's being excised and being removed. And I think people are upset about it and fed up with it.

"Everyone would agree that there should not be a national religion. There should not be a theocracy. You certainly don't want to have a national religion, but to say that that translates into having to deny what our history is, having to deny that religion is very much a part of our culture. I mean, the one doesn't translate into the other.

"The purpose of the establishment clause was to ensure that we didn't have a theocracy, that we had a democratic form of government, and that we didn't have a religious form of government. But we're a Christian nation, and we're certainly a religious people. And religion has very much been a part of our history, part of our culture. It has been, and will continue to be.

"I think we're doing an absolute disservice to the education of our kids when we want to remove religion as one of the threads of education."

JEFF VENTRELLA, DIRECTOR, NATIONAL LITIGATION ACADEMY, ALLIANCE DEFENSE FUND, PHOENIX, ARIZONA

Jeff Ventrella graduated from the University of California's Hastings School of Law in San Francisco in 1985. He has been in practice twenty years, having first been involved in corporate law and environmental law and later in Christian litigation. He was hired by the Alliance Defense Fund to run their National Litigation Academy, its Regional Litigation Academies, and the training for Christian legal students, called the Blackstone Legal Fellowship. The Alliance Defense Fund steps in when it sees a school district or municipal government is engaged in viewpoint discrimination against Christians, very often at Christmas. All train volunteer lawyers to go out and challenge the ACLU when it comes to court trying to shut down religious freedom.

Ventrella is from Boise, Idaho; he is forty-six years old. His father was a professional musician, and he learned to play trumpet at an early age. By the time he was eleven years old he was playing professionally, and eventually went to music school. That was all before he changed his mind and went to law school.

"No Supreme Court, no federal court has said you can't sing a hymn, a Christmas carol in a public school," said Ventrella. "That's just a mischaracterization on the state of the law. Many, many school districts, there's thousands of them, are accountable fiscally, and they've got to make sure that the budgetary issues line up. With the budget cuts and those kinds of economic pressures, combined with a threatening e-mail or a letter that has ACLU on it which tells people, If you do this, you will be sued, the first thing the administrator, who's had no training in constitutional law, does is say to himself, 'You know what, I can avoid this, I can head it off by just saying, "I don't have to do any of this stuff, it's just easier to not."'

"I think that there has been a successful, though not accurate, but a successful campaign to misinform. And there's this kind of white noise in the air, in which people say, 'That must be the law, yeah, that must be the law.' People begin to get kowtowed. A couple cases get publicized, and people begin to extrapolate from those cases and say, 'Yeah, I guess that's the law.' Rather than looking at the myriad of decisions that clearly contradict the censors out there who try to suppress Christmas.

"The ACLU is the main opponent in this area, on the Christmas issue, absolutely, yes. Both from the top, President Nadine Strossen, all the way down to the various local chapters. They are the ones who have repeatedly led the anti-Christmas effort. The secondary folks would be people like Americans United for Separation of Church and State and People for the American Way. But clearly, with the litigation clout, it's the ACLU.

"The reality is, their legal position is extremely weak; it's rarely sustained when it's challenged. What the ACLU has going for it is a reputation and a war chest and the threat. Most people respond to that, even if they don't have to do it. It's a form of shaming or a form of intimidation, if you will.

"Most lawyers stumbled through constitutional law in law school, and they didn't study it except to pass the bar. The laws have changed. The laws have been, frankly, much more invigorated for religious expression in the public square. And so you have a lawyer who's really using either dated impressions or secondary sources or, worse yet, relying on the ACLU's version of the law to make that advice to their clients. And so you don't really have informed constitutional litigators who know the state of the law.

"I believe that people are beginning to realize that abdication is not the answer. I think that this last year and a half there's been a real touchstone. 'You know what? Enough is enough.' And people are beginning to get energized to the idea that, hey, we *can* celebrate Christmas.

"We're not subclass citizens to want to celebrate Christmas. You don't even have to be particularly religious; it can be a cultural expressiveness, and there's nothing constitutionally infirm about that. So what I see happening are countermeasures beginning to develop and getting organized.

"Basically the notion of Christmas law is a subset of what's called 'viewpoint discrimination.' That's the technical part of the law. We have a number of hours that are devoted to how to litigate civil rights claims and, in particular, viewpoint discriminatory claims. We have something called the Christmas Project. So once a lawyer goes through this intense week of training, including those four hours of intense training on viewpoint discrimination, and public forum doctrines, then we have the Christmas Project. What that does is train lawyers full bore on media, op-ed, and litigation letters as well as litigation pleadings. All that is available to our allies to get involved and get embedded in this particular issue, whether that's through media appearances, whether it's through writing op-ed pieces, or actually representing clients in stopping the anti-Christmas onslaught, standing in the gap.

"It's been very successful, [there's] high participation by our trained lawyers to do this. And, again, it shows us that the answer is more often than not showing up, rather than having the big gun, because the ACLU's position is a house of cards legally.

"Well, we train about fifty at a time, and to date we've trained over eight hundred. Then we can rally them through the Christmas Project. But even if it is eight hundred, it's relatively small compared to the army of ACLU lawyers.

"The Christmas Project-allied attorneys participated in this. Our allied attorneys sent letters to seven thousand school districts; the year before we had sent one thousand. These letters reached fifty thousand school districts.

"I was actually recruited by the Alliance Defense Fund. I fit the profile that they wanted, to beef up the training component. They wanted someone who had competent litigation skill, I mean real lawyering kind of stuff. And they also wanted someone who had philosophical and theological acumen to design and run some of these programs. Not just from a pragmatic standpoint, but from a strategic standpoint. And I kind of fit that bill.

"I think they're also understanding that public interest law was intrinsically Christian. Most people have lost that. Most people have thought that when they hear public interest law they think of Sierra Club, ACLU, People for the American Way, NAACP, all of which are involved in that. But it didn't start there. Public interest law started clear back, frankly, when John the Baptist said, You can't take your brother's wife. He went into the public square and talked about the design of marriage. Of course, he got beheaded because of it."

JORDAN LORENCE, ALLIANCE DEFENSE FUND, PHOENIX, ARIZONA

Jordan Lorence has been an employee of the Alliance Defense Fund of Phoenix, Arizona, for four years. He moved to Phoenix in 2002, after living in Washington, D.C., for eighteen years. He is originally from Mile, Minnesota, original home of Tonka Toys. He just turned fifty, he and his wife have been married twenty years, and they have seven children.

"I think that it is that there are people whose sentiments about religion are simply offended on a deep intellectual level. They just feel religion is a crutch. It's used by people of lesser intelligence, and that they just want to see it expunged. And then I also think that there's some sort of pride issue on being the zealous enforcer of the First Amendment, and the way that people can be offended by the most ordinary Christmas thing to me is astonishing.

"The whole concept of freedom of speech is that you should be able to tolerate opinions you disagree with even if they're stated by the government. And to sing 'Silent Night' at a choir concert or something like that is not something that is going to tear the Republic in half so that we should have to abolish it. Now, people who object, who belong to some non-Christian religion, of course should not be required to sing a Christmas carol or participate. But for them to say, 'Well, I am offended so I want it censored for everybody,' to me is an overkill application of the establishment clause of the Constitution.

"This has crept into the jurisprudence of the establishment clause mainly by Sandra Day O'Connor. She wrote in the 1984 *Lynch* v. *Donnelly* case about the nativity scene, about when religion is used by the government in a way that people of nonadherence perceive themselves to be outsiders.

"Now what happened is groups like the ACLU have taken this to mean that anybody who's offended by anything with the least little religious content can run into court and get an injunction censoring this. These two Ten Commandments cases for example: the one in Texas, a guy just walked by the Ten Commandments monument by the state capitol in Texas every day on his way to the law library. He said, 'I'm offended by it.' Why do we allow these people with *eggshell* sensitivity to obliterate all this stuff? And I think the courts are beginning to question now, 'Why are we allowing these offended observers so much leeway in court when if we had any other message [they claimed to be offended about] we wouldn't even give [them] the time of day.'

"We've gotten this imbalance where non-Christian religious stuff is viewed as cultural. So therefore it never violates the establishment clause. And Christian stuff is viewed as religious, so it does violate the establishment clause.

"We are right now engaged in this major lawsuit against the New York City Department of Education, which has basically said, 'Everybody, all the community groups, can rent school facilities on nights and weekends except for worship groups.' So we got a preliminary injunction [which allows worship groups the same access] and you would have thought that the barbarians have overrun the gates of the city the way they wailed.

"And the rhetoric isn't overtly hostile, but it is definitely along the lines, 'We don't want these people in our neighborhoods.' There's now twenty-three evangelical Christian churches meeting [in New York school buildings] out of almost 1,200 school buildings in New York City. And you would think the Huns have overrun the city, like in ancient Rome. I just think that there's kind of this secularist, well-educated mind-set that's used against people who take their religions seriously, unless it's like the Dalai Lama, unless it's some exotic religion that not that many people believe in. Whether traditional Catholic, Orthodox Jew, evangelical Christian . . . it just sends them up the wall. They have feelings of disdain, loathing, and contempt and fear at the same time."

KELLY SHACKELFORD, LIBERTY LEGAL INSTITUTE, PLANO, TEXAS

Kelly Shackelford founded Liberty Legal Institute in 1997 to fight for the protection of religious freedoms and First Amendment rights for individuals, groups, and churches. Shackelford clerked for a federal judge after law school.

"When their freedoms are taken away, the average person isn't O. J. Simpson and can't just go out and hire the dream team. My heart has always been to make sure that those people have the best representation possible so that the government can't erode all of our freedoms by picking on the people who don't have the money to fight.

"Religion is the new pornography. If somebody says something religious, the average government official feels like he or she has to run from the room, screaming with their hair on fire. Religion is treated like pornography would be treated if you brought it into the school. I mean, there's a fear. There's a shame, almost, directed toward it.

"The ACLU is mainly operating on remote control. They've injected this chilling atmosphere that's antireligious in the schools and they don't even have to do anything in most instances to effectuate a religious cleansing in the schools. They've managed to scare and intimidate and the lore in school districts is religion is bad, religion will get you in trouble.

"I'd say a decent percentage of the time, the person who engages in the violation of our clients' rights is somebody who later will tell us, 'I'm a religious person.' They just didn't know any better, and what they're doing is reacting. They go to the knee-jerk, shut-it-down action. 'Oh, it's religion? We must shut it down.' That is the general approach.

"These are young kids. They're in third grade or fourth grade or fifth grade. And the lesson they learn is there are words you can't say. You can't say these curse words, and then you can't say your religion. You can't talk about your religion. And it's a very powerful message.

"We had a case where the kids could could draw a tracing of their foot, then put a message on the drawing of their foot, and then put it up on the board in class. And all these kids had all these very innocuous messages, 'Jenny loves Johnny' and 'Peace' and such. A girl very innocently wrote 'Jesus Loves Me.' And the teacher ripped it down, and said to her, 'Don't you ever do this again.' The girl went home crying and wondering what she'd done wrong.

"The father was just infuriated. We called the school. And that time, the school had already realized they were in big trouble. And so they went back to this little girl and they told her, unbeknownst to any of us, 'Go ahead and do another—go ahead and do another one and put it up.' She redrew her foot. And instead of writing 'Jesus Loves Me' in the innocent and pure way she did before, she put a little tiny cross up in the very top corner that you could just barely see.

"And I thought, 'There's the picture of what happens inside to these little kids.' She's learned the lesson. Don't be open about your faith. Don't be honest about your faith. Hide it. You can still be whoever you are as long as you'll hide it. They taught her self-oppression and self-censorship through this hysterical reaction to her. They robbed her of that innocence and of that purity of being open about her faith.

"That's the sort of thing I decided to fight."

HIRAM SASSER, LIBERTY LEGAL INSTITUTE, PLANO, TEXAS

Thirty-year-old Hiram Sasser intended to be a military lawyer. At Oklahoma State University he joined the Reserve Officer Training Corps (ROTC) and eventually went to law school at the same university because he was offered a scholarship. "I got paid to go to law school," he says. His original intention was to go into corporate law, after a stint in the army as a Judge Advocate General (JAG) lawyer. A ruptured disk in his lower back ended his military career, and he decided constitutional law was another way to serve the country.

"The government is required by the Constitution to tolerate the speech of individuals even if it is religious viewpoint or religiously motivated speech.

"Even if it offends others the government still has to tolerate it. In the history of the latter part of the twentieth century it's been a story of different steps leading to a banishment of religious speech. Step one was to make sure that there's no government endorsement of religion.

"Step two was to make sure that all ideas are acceptable no matter how ridiculous, such as the notion there is no absolute truth, that everything is relative.

"Step three is where they trip you up by saying 'Except for all ideas are not equal, we don't like your ideas and we'll label them as intolerant.'

"What's given rise to a lot of the litigation in the past ten years is the religious folks striking back and saying we've had this long enough. We're not going to be discriminated against.

"For several years it has been reported to us by parents that in this particular school district in Plano, Texas, the students and the parents who contributed things to the so-called holiday party were not allowed to bring anything that was red or green. The rules said items such as plates and napkins could only be white. So the district was banning red and green.

"When we had a hearing for a restraining order in federal court, the judge was courteous enough not to laugh at the school district about that. But he made a special note at the hearing to tell the parents and kids that they could bring red and green plates and napkins if they wanted to.

"What we're doing is simply saying the students have free speech rights and even have free speech rights when they're at school. These speech rights can only be overcome if they're causing a material and substantial disruption. If you're not causing any trouble why should you be punished? We're saying, 'Look, they can speak about religion. They can share their religious faith with their friends. They can do it written form, or in verbal form.'

"As long as they're not causing a disruption, if somebody is offended that doesn't count."

BILL DONOHUE, THE CATHOLIC LEAGUE, NEW YORK CITY

Bill Donohue is included in this list of prominent Christian litigators even though he is not a lawyer. He's just been fighting liberal and left-wing lawyers, most prominently the ACLU, most of his adult life. He holds a Ph.D. in sociology and has been a college professor and a high school teacher in New York City. He wrote his doctoral dissertation on the American Civil Liberties Union and, unlike virtually every person now active in the

ACLU, he actually spoke with—conducted an interview with—the late Roger Baldwin, who founded the ACLU in 1920 and whose thinking and philosophy guides the ACLU even today. Donohue interviewed him when Baldwin was in his late eighties in 1978. Donohue has been an implacable foe of the ACLU when it comes to issues of religion in the public square and many ACLU positions on religion are derived directly from Baldwin. I interviewed Donohue at length in early 2005.

"The ACLU takes a radical secularist understanding of religion in the public square. And as far as they're concerned, to the extent that Christianity in particular, but not exclusively, has influence in American society we are less free as a people. They look at freedom as anathema to liberty, unlike Tocqueville, who understood, in his work *Democracy in America,* that religion was the cradle of liberty. They would reject that wholesale. So as far as they're concerned, the more we can have religion recede from public life, the freer our society will be.

"The ACLU being the legal arm of the liberal left, they entertain the secularist vision of freedom. And so as far as they're concerned, if we can war on Christmas, and by that I mean that we can expel from public life any celebrations of Christmas, we are going to be a freer society as a result.

"The ACLU has not won every case before the courts. The courts have been much more accommodationist than the ACLU would understand. So in order to understand really why our society has this public space animus against religion, you have to look at how our culture has been affected by the ACLU elites. And that is to say, if you'll take a look at the educational establishments, and if you take a look at the corporations, particularly in the diversity offices, what you're going to see is we have a multicultural ideology in our society, which on the face of it sounds benign.

"What you really have is an intersection here of elites in our society who are overwhelmingly men and women on the left who have a particular animus against the public expression of religion. They're found in the academy, they're found in the corporate world, and they're found certainly amongst the legal activist organizations. And unless they are resisted, they will continue to trample on the public expression of religion.

"In 1989, in Harrisburg, Pennsylvania, an ACLU lawyer, on his lunch break, went over to the rotunda of the state capitol to inspect a Christmas tree with about a thousand ornaments. He said that he found about three of them that were in the shape of a cross. Now, these ornaments had been made by senior citizens in the Harrisburg, Pennsylvania, area. He immediately went into federal district court to get those crosses removed. It was thrown out, thank God. But the point is this: The same ACLU which will defend as freedom of expression Andre Serrano, who takes a crucifix and puts it in a jar of his own urine, they will defend that as freedom of speech. So here what we have is this kind of paradox.

"An ACLU lawyer looking at a Christmas tree in a government building will object to the display of a crucifix unless it has been defamed and put into a jar of urine or feces. Then, all of a sudden it symbolically becomes art, and therefore it's entitled to First Amendment protection under freedom of speech. That is exactly where we have come to today.

"People are offended. We have this every single year. We have schools who say, 'Well, we want to treat everyone equally, so therefore Jews are allowed the menorah, the Muslims are allowed the crescent and star, and Christians are allowed the Christmas tree.' That would be on the order of saying, 'Well, the Christian gets the nativity scene and the Jews get the dreidel.' Well, that wouldn't be fair, Jews wouldn't put up with that, nor should they. They'd say, 'Wait a minute, if Christians are getting the real thing, the nativity scene, why are we getting a quasisecular symbol in the dreidel? We want the menorah, which symbolizes a miracle.'

"If a Catholic is offended by a star of David, or a crescent and star, wouldn't the right corrective be to educate the Catholic and get him out of his dim-wittedness and his bigotry?

"What we are talking about here, in all of these cases, is censorship, and that is the word that must be used. ACLU people say, 'Oh no, we're in favor of freedom of speech.' Yes, freedom of speech for child pornographers, freedom of speech for mud wrestlers, freedom of speech for dwarf tossing, taking a dwarf and throwing him in a bar across the room."

But not for Christians.

CHAPTER 9

THE WAR ON CHRISTIANS

What I have learned is that the war on Christmas is worse than I thought. Not only because it's going on in red states, where you'd least expect diversity witch hunts to take place. And not only because its liberal foot soldiers have gone further than the Supreme Court in banning Christmastime.

The war on Christmas is worse than I thought—and perhaps than you thought, because it's really a war on Christianity. In all the dramas described here that have played out over bans on the public celebration of Christmas, the plaintiff's reason is always that Christmas is Christian, and symbols of Christianity can't be permitted in public places.

In today's America, one is hard-pressed to find instances of Judaism suppressed in the schools, or in the workplace. Even in a post–9/11 world, Islam is treated so tenderly that the traditionally Polish Catholic enclave of Hamtramck, Michigan, altered its noise ordinance to allow local mosques to blast the Muslim call to prayer from loudspeakers.

Anti-Christian bias is often casual and often doesn't recognize itself in the mirror, as we see in the chapter on the city of Eugene.

There it was explicitly stated in complaints about Christmas that the offending Christmas trees were just too Christian. It took a tidal wave of protest for City Manager Jim Johnson (whose wife and family had to decamp to Portland for a few days, for safety's sake), an otherwise agreeable person, to realize that he had been lured into the war against Christians.

After reading up on Christmas-related decisions by the Supreme Court of the United States, Johnson changed his own ruling, and the following year officially permitted the display of Christmas trees again in a few public spaces controlled by his office. Some of Johnson's associates and subordinates, while still smarting from the Christian smack down, nonetheless continue to think they were right in removing the Christmas trees, and in their sullen acceptance of the return of Christmas trees seem to think Christians are out of control and need to be suppressed.

Five years after Jim Johnson's Christmas tree fight a letter to the editor appeared in the Eugene *Register-Guard* complaining about Christians. Eugene resident Anne Cutting objected to Christians putting signs on the front lawns of their homes at Easter.

Editor:

I am mystified over the sprouting of signs reading "Easter—Jesus, He is Risen." It seems confrontational to me, or messianic at the least.

We all hold deeply felt beliefs, and since this is a free country we can express them any way we wish, but I wonder if I placed any of the following messages on my front yard—"Abortion Rights," "Gay Rights," the Star of David, "Right to Life," "Black Power," "God Bless George Bush" or "Impeach

George Bush"—if they would offend anyone. Of course they would.

Our gender or religious preferences should be private matters, not advertised on our lawns. Has religion descended into the political arena with signs about which side we're on? Doesn't that demean one's faith?

Maybe someone can explain the purpose of the signs.

Anne Cutting, Eugene

Ms. Cutting and Jim Johnson and others have something in common: They seemed to have forgotten that free speech is a religious right as well as a political right. The founders of this nation were religionists—Christian—and they were smarting from the imposition of two official religions in the early days of the country. First was the Puritans, who actually forbade the celebration of Christmas. Cotton Mather, the Puritan leader at Plymouth, allowed Christmas to be observed only if it happened to fall on Sunday, the day of church services. The next official religion was the Anglican church, which was forced upon the colonists by the king following the fall of Oliver Cromwell and the Puritans. Americans didn't like either official religion, and established the right to speak freely about religion as a basic, inalienable right.

Ms. Cutting needs to be educated (to use the parlance of liberals) and taught that free speech also means the obligation of others, such as herself, to tolerate speech they do not like.

Cutting seems to be turned off by the Christian mission to carry the good news of Jesus Christ, a mission held in common by both Protestants and Catholics (though conservative evangelicals are often considered the only ones who proselytize).

Maybe some people still don't get it: The central tenet of 84 percent of the country's religion is evangelization, which requires free speech in public. The few Christians who do not evangelize do not negate the point.

I don't think people like Cutting are actually asking a question and expecting an answer when they inquire, What is the purpose of those signs? Deeply embedded in the cocoon of her rhetorical question is hostility to Christians. She doesn't want to see or hear their religion at all. She wants them to take their religion inside, indoors and out of sight, practiced as if it were sex, in the privacy of one's own home, or in private churches.

That attitude demonstrates a desire on her part, and evidently on the part of others who feel like she does, to push Christianity into a place where it does not confront people, where it is hidden. Liberal crusaders are treating Christianity as if it were second-hand smoke from cigarettes: segregate it, hide it, and wherever you can . . . ban it. To this point, there's a popular bumper sticker spotted around Eugene, Oregon, these days that reads "So Many Christians, So Few Lions."

Secular humanist hostility to Christianity is not merely a joking bumper sticker demonstrating a willingness to be outrageous, but a deeply felt hostility toward Christians that wouldn't be tolerated against other world religions. Can you imagine, "So Many Jews . . . " or, "So Many Muslims . . ."?

Of course not. But it's open season on the constitutional rights of Christians.

In doing research for this book I continued to come across amateur constitutional law practitioners who got way out ahead of the Supreme Court of the United States when it came to banning Christmas. They were treating the separation of church and state rulings currently on the books like the basic model of a new car, like they're there to be loaded up with extra features and upgrades.

The Supreme Court of the United States (SCOTUS) has made many rulings with which many Christians disagree. For instance, it is by no means universally accepted that the nativity scene, the crèche, ought to be categorized as an impermissible religious symbol. There is no question that it is a religious symbol, but Christians argue that it should not be forbidden in a public setting, as the Supreme Court has ruled. Other religions are allowed to display their faith-oriented symbols in public without complaint, usually as proof of community "inclusiveness" and "diversity."

"The Jews get a menorah, a religious symbol that signifies a miracle," said Bill Donohue of the Catholic League, "the Muslims get the star and crescent, which signifies the miracle of the prophet, and what do Christians get? A tree? Come on! Christians want the real thing too. We want the crèche, which signifies the miracle of the birth of Jesus Christ."

The courts have also produced other rulings involving the public display of the Christian cross that have angered Christians. Presently, for instance, the federal appellate courts are insisting on the removal of a crude wooden cross set on a lonely promontory of desert in Nevada at the end of the Korean War, which has been tended by a succession of military veterans. The cross overlooks a highway slicing through bare Nevada hills, but it is federal land. Not only do the secularists and the courts want the cross off federal land, they want it gone for good. Both have resisted all efforts to transfer the small piece of federally owned land the cross sits on to a private entity, in order to disentangle church and state.

No. The cross must come down, they insist.

Christians have objections measured in the metric ton when it comes to SCOTUS and its religious rulings. But it makes it so much worse when the liberal plot to ban Christmas piles more restrictions on top of the Court's.

The Supreme Court of the United States has never said a Christmas tree is unconstitutional, it has never said the singing of Christmas carols is unconstitutional, it has never said the greeting Merry Christmas is unconstitutional, it has never said Santa Claus is unconstitutional, it has never said using the word "Christmas" on a public document is unconstitutional. But the secularists merrily declare all these Christmas symbols banned, precisely because these symbols are Christian.

The northern California chapter of the American Civil Liberties Union addressed this precise issue on its own Web site, in a section of frequently asked questions. One question was whether it was permissible in schools to display the list of Christmas symbols I've just mentioned (Christmas tree, Santa, etc.). The answer from the ACLU was honest to a point. It said, yes, these items may be displayed according to the law, but teachers should think about whether they should go ahead and do what the law allows or if they should instead make diversity and inclusivity primary goals and ban Christmas altogether. In this construction, inclusion of all requires exclusion of all even remotely Christian religious symbols. It was the same argument given by Professor Roisman at the Indiana School of Law when she insisted that a Christmas tree should come down: "It's not a matter of law, it's a matter of policy," she wrote. In other words, even though we have lost the legal argument, we shall persist because we want to push the law farther.

In which direction? In the direction of more restriction, more censorship of Christmas and Christian religious symbols for the purpose of removing Christianity from public view.

In the stories of Baldwin City, Kansas, and Covington, Georgia, the American Civil Liberties Union was a major player in the banning of Christmas symbols. In one case it was Santa Claus who was banished; in the other case it was the very word "Christmas," but in both cases the complaints were that the word and the symbols conveyed Christianity, which simply could not and should not be tolerated. What is a child to think, except that the Christian religion is not welcome, is not tolerated, is to be pushed out of the public arena because there is something wrong with it? Because it oppresses or excludes others?

In both cases the ACLU lawyer stated that the presence of Christian symbols, and therefore Christianity itself, was intolerable. In both cases, the ACLU lawyer took the position that if the Christian religion were acknowledged by an official person or an official group of people (a school board, for instance) an absolutely impermissible concept would have been allowed to enter public discussion: Christianity itself.

In Covington, Georgia, the ACLU lawyer, Craig Goodmark, actually argued to me that simply acknowledging that the school was taking two weeks off for Christmas would coerce students into the practice of Christianity. "The practical problem with it is that children are people that live in Covington and Newton County and are entitled to go to these schools and not be, I say exposed, but not be coerced into participating in a Christmas holiday." When you stop to think about it, that is a stunning argument, a really breathtaking position, yet Goodmark was not engaged in hyperbole. It was, evidently, his understanding of the position of the Atlanta, Georgia, chapter of the American Civil

Liberties Union. One could infer that that position appears to regard Christianity as so toxic students must not be subjected to even the slightest whiff of it.

Of course, in Covington, Georgia, the offense committed by a school board member was more than simply wanting the Christmas break to be called what it actually is. His offense was saying out loud that America is a Christian nation.

Gee, it sure feels like a Christian country, when 84 percent of those polled identify themselves as Christian and 96 percent say they celebrate Christmas. But you're not allowed to say it.

Along with plainly racist statements and grotesquely sexual innuendo, that is probably the single most forbidden sentence in American English today. For the sharp-eyed secularists who look for intention in every word of people they believe to be Christian, saying that this is a Christian nation is tantamount to saying, "So the rest of you, get out." The secularists who desperately wish this were *not* a Christian nation find that statement scandalous. There is no doubt they would like America to be something else, perhaps a nation of atheists. But their wishes do not make it so, and as an observational matter the United States of America is a Christian country, and the huge numbers of new arrivals from other countries and other cultures have not changed that fact to any great degree.

Christians of all stripes played an enormous roll in the 2004 election, giving John Kerry the electoral ability to make the election relatively close, but also giving George W. Bush the extra electoral oomph to clearly carry the day.

Nonbelievers, Jews, Muslims, Hindus, all non-Christians amount to a total of no more than 15 percent, but considering how non-Christians shatter into different belief and nonbelief factions, they are even less effective in creating the political sway that their overall number would indicate.

However, that relatively small population of non-Christians seems to have convinced a great many Christians that Christianity is too big, too powerful, too overwhelming, and that Christians should put Christianity in a secondary position to make room for other, minor religionists, and for nonbelievers.

But again, it's not adherents of lesser represented religions who are banning Christmas. Their numbers are too small. Sadly, there is no other explanation for the success of anti-Christmas and anti-Christian forces than that it is due to liberal, guilt-wracked Christians who are embarrassed that they are in the majority. Otherwise, the numbers do not add up. We saw that phenomena in the chapter on Jim Johnson, the city manager in Eugene. He is a practicing Christian, and evidently a guilt-wracked Christian.

We saw it in the experience of Dean Anthony Tarr at Indiana School of Law, who is also a practicing Episcopalian. Tony Tarr inadvertently provoked a tremendous fight on his campus by falling victim to empty arguments of inclusiveness, and of the exclusionary practices of Christmas. These arguments rest on the notion that when religion is practiced by adherents a nonparticipant is not included, or may feel excluded, and therefore there is something wrong with the practice of the religion in public.

By this notion Jews in Israel should cease their religious practices, because by definition Muslim Arabs are excluded. By this notion Muslims in Hamtramck, Michigan, should not issue the call to prayer over public loudspeakers because Christians would feel excluded. Christians are sometimes annoyed in Hamtramck, but there has been no problem there among different religionists in the year or more that mosques have been broadcasting the call to prayer for all to hear, whether Muslim or not. The city oblig-ingly changed a noise ordinance to accommodate the religious observance of a large population of newly arrived Muslims, and the Muslim call to prayer is heard five times a day.

When Jews practice their religion in public, does an Anne Cutting complain? Do we see objections to the yarmulke as "con-frontational" or "messianic" because we see Jews wearing it in public?

No. The complaints about religion being practiced in public are almost exclusively about Christianity. Occasionally, a Jewish organization like the Anti-Defamation League will object to a Jewish religious practice that is carried out under public auspices, but in my opinion the objection is lodged only to maintain the rhetorical standing to object to Christian practices. Thus, the ADL opposed school holidays for Rosh Hashanah and Yom Kip-pur a few years ago in a predominantly Jewish school district.

In Mustang, Oklahoma, we see the effect of legal advice ig-nited by an ACLU objection and driven by a fear of litigation. Somehow many lawyers representing school districts have come to believe that the courts have said that there will be no religion-connected holiday celebrations in schools whatsoever. There has never been such a ruling from the United States Supreme Court, and it is mythology created by the ACLU and others that has convinced even lawyers that there are such decisions. Superinten-dent Karl Springer learned the hard way that the easiest thing to do is pay attention to key court decisions. In those rulings he learned to avoid the temptation to ban all conceivably religious references in school activities or curriculum, but instead to teach about various faiths.

When Springer was attacked after his decision to ban a nativity scene and the singing of "Silent Night" (the song was not banned—an erroneous newspaper report, as it turned out) he provoked an outcry that was similar to the anger expressed in other towns where the de-Christianizing process had come into public view. Those who speak out in public meetings, hold protests, give interviews to the media very often are objecting to the atmosphere of hostility and are not usually the type who want their religion taught as devotional lessons in schools. The backlash usually comes from people who believe that such draconian, censorial steps as Springer took actually teach a lesson of hostility to young children about their religion.

But in the end, Mustang, Oklahoma, had to be rescued by a liberal advocacy group based in the South, which embraces faith in a red state manner that mainline leftists often find abhorrent. Here a lonely voice of the left was teaching a lesson in how to allow religious symbols (such as those of Christmas) into the school as educational features of the curriculum and not as Sunday school lessons that more properly belong in church.

Charles Haynes and the First Amendment Center rushed to assure that they are not lawyers. They do not litigate; they negotiate. In Mustang, Oklahoma, the pastor of the largest evangelical church agreed to the Haynes-inspired plan and publicly endorsed it.

It is not the approach of the ACLU, which is more typical of liberal and leftist thinking when it comes to religion in public. However, even in places where the ACLU is weak, such as Texas, the secularist philosophy has become woven into the very fabric of the public schools.

In Plano, Texas, the school district was so certain that a few parents wanted to take over the school with Christianity that the district thought the only way to resist was to keep all Christianity out. Plano is emblematic of the depth of the problem, because it is one of a handful of school districts that had actually banned the colors red and green.

"It's just absolutely ludicrous to me to tell somebody you can't wrap a package in green and red at Christmas time. I mean, how silly and petty and small can you be?" asked Reverend Jack Graham, founder and head of the Prestonwood Baptist Church, the megachurch located in Plano. He told me he was shocked at the degree to which the school district was willing to act to suppress Christian practices.

"You have to think, if someone is willing to go to that extreme to suppress Christian tradition, Christian faith, then there must be an aggressive agenda coming from somebody somewhere. I just don't know who it is."

It is worth noting that the Shaker Heights City School District where Peter Horoschak had served as superintendent was also one of a few that have banned red and green, and now Horoschak runs the Maplewood, New Jersey, school district, where we probably have the most glaring example of liberal Christianity suppressing or censoring itself.

Dr. Peter Horoschak's actions regarding Christmas are perceived by many to be anti-Christian. When it comes to schools, he is also openly and overtly antireligion generally. He has been a school superintendent a long time, and he knows all the arguments for teaching certain religious holidays in the classroom, but he has decided that what may be right, correct, or legal under the Constitution actually cannot be accomplished in what would be a fair and equitable manner. So if it can't be done fairly, Horoschak's view is it's best not to do anything connected to religion at all.

That has led to a total scrub down of Christmas from every

school district he's ever led. In Albuquerque, New Mexico, where he stopped briefly between stints in Shaker Heights, Ohio, and Maplewood, New Jersey, he got into a public dispute with the Navajo tribe over the wearing of native dress. He also fired a music director who defied orders to remove all Christmas music from performance programs.

Dr. Horoschak might be unusual. There may not be many school superintendents whose outlook on the running of the schools is so thoroughly colored by his personal family situation, as Horoschak, who has children and grandchildren of diverse racial background. Dr. Horoschak's approach is that the school should be apart from the calendar of the outside world: Inside the schoolhouse walls there is no Christmas, there is no Ramadan, there is no Yom Kippur, there is no Diwali, and the reason is because there are so many others lurking in the wings poised to assert themselves, to demand a place in the school if he were to allow access to even one of them.

Dr. Horoschak's attitude and philosophy come from a much earlier time than today. In a fine book of Christmas scholarship called *The December Wars* author Albert Menendez rediscovered the great boycott and walkout of New York City schools in 1907. In that year, Jewish students had decided they'd had enough of the constant Protestant indoctrination of the New York City schools, and they staged a mass boycott and walkout of the schools in protest. The Jewish students, an overwhelmingly large proportion of the school population, refused to come back to school until the lessons and assemblies ratcheted back on the overt Protestant indoctrination of the school curriculum. The Jewish students won. The New York schools became largely nonsectarian as of 1908.

That was a good victory, and almost anybody today would agree. But that general agreement among various religionists, even the majority Christians, has been used to advance the cause of nonsectarian schools into the theater of the absurd, as we have seen. In some cases it has been used to carry out an agenda of suppressing and locking out Christianity altogether.

This needn't be so.

A good example of how the schools don't have to operate this way is in the Finger Lakes district of upstate New York, where the Canandaigua City School District superintendent is an eighteen-year veteran named Steven Uebbing.

Uebbing and his school district made the news in 2004 as well. A principal in his district sent out a memo directing staff to cease using the greeting Merry Christmas, and declaring that overt Christian Christmas symbols would be banned from use in the schools. Uebbing immediately issued a news release of his own correcting the record: "Christmas is not banned in the Canandaigua School District," Uebbing said, unequivocally.

Uebbing has quite a bit of experience in dealing with the issue of being fair at Christmas to both Christians and non-Christians.

"There came a time when a group of non-Christian parents of very young children, kindergartners and first-graders specifically, were concerned that the sentiment in the classroom was so focused just on Christmas and not anything else, that their kids felt excluded," Uebbing said in an interview with me recorded in the spring of 2005. "And so we looked into this and we found that there were times where some of the things that were happening in the classroom would exclude kids."

Correctly, he believes exclusionary practices in the schools should be avoided. Uebbing's philosophy of running schools, especially schools in the lowest grades, is to make sure that no kid has a bad day in school because he or she feels excluded.

"I'll give you a perfect example," Uebbing said. "A teacher sends home a homework assignment for kindergarten kids, and the homework assignment is to sit down with your parents and talk about all the things, all the steps that your family went through to select, buy, and decorate this year's Christmas tree."

Uebbing teaches education law as an adjunct professor at a nearby college. He is well aware of the Supreme Court decisions on what can and can't go on in schools at Christmastime, according to interpretations of the Constitution by the Court. His teacher's misjudgment was not a federal case exactly, but at best such an assignment appeared to be a little thoughtless.

"If you come home in a Jewish family, it's tough to do that assignment. So the parents complained to the assistant principal, who by the way happens to be an evangelical Christian himself. He says, 'Well, that shouldn't be, kids shouldn't feel excluded in the class.' So he called a group of teachers together and said, 'What can we do about this?' And they said, 'Well, we don't want anybody feeling left out. This is a public school, it's not a Christian school.'" To make certain little children feel part of everything going on in the school, the teachers made some rules for themselves.

"So they came up with a list of ideas. If you have Christmas decorations up, let's put some Hanukah decorations up. If you're going to have a party, let's make it a holiday party. Let's make sure that all the kids feel that this is their classroom, not just the classroom for the Christian kids."

OK, but you don't mean put up symbols of the Jewish religion, or the Muslim religion, but ban Christian symbols? Thankfully he did not.

"In our district, every school had a Christmas tree at the time, and we still do. Every school has a concert, and most of the music is Christmas music. There's usually a couple of other songs there, to be more representative of the holiday season for the kids who may not be the dominant population. It's always gone well; we've never had a complaint of any kind."

So in Uebbing's district, Christmas is in, and Hanukah is in.

"People would go to our concerts and hear the rendition of 'Silent Night,' and say, 'Geez, I heard you guys weren't doing that this year.' I said, 'Of course we're doing it, we're not restricting things.' We never had a single person come to a board meeting and protest this."

Uebbing accepts that it is part of his job to educate kids about history and music and art, even if the lessons must teach something about religion. It's a bit of a juggling act, but he thinks his job is to juggle.

Why not just force it all out of the school? Why not make certain no one feels left out, no one feels uncomfortable by simply eliminating any and all references to anybody's religion from the schools entirely? Why not take the approach of Dr. Peter Horoschak in the Maplewood, New Jersey, school district?

"Education law has changed. This is the other thing you have to remember. It's changed dramatically religiouswise.

"So when you get people who have had their training in the late eighties and early nineties they often have a stilted view of the church and state issue, that 'separation' is exactly what the policy must be in terms of the role of the public school. But that doesn't mean that you have to prohibit all religious expression in public schools, especially when it's the expression of the nonschool actors, meaning students, the kids themselves. Teachers and teachers' aides . . . their speech is somewhat controlled, but the kids' speech is free speech, even if it involves religious issues."

It is on that point that the Plano school district went so wrong and demonstrated anti-Christian bias. Part of the policy of the Plano Independent School District was to make an effort to enforce a rule against students giving other students anything that could be considered a religious message. One of the plaintiffs in the Plano case, the eight-year-old student named Jonathan Morgan, wanted to give his classmates a gift, a candy cane ink pen and a note attached that told the "Legend of the Candy Cane." It was an overtly religious message about Jesus Christ, and the school prohibited it for precisely that reason: It was a Christian message.

An exact duplicate of the same situation was occurring at about the same time in a school district in Massachusetts, and in that case the Bush Justice Department entered the case on the side of the student, asserting that student-to-student communication is free speech and cannot be stopped by the school officials. Joining the Bush Justice Department on the side of the student in that case was the Massachusetts ACLU.

The local chapter of the American Civil Liberties Union saw the case as a pure free speech issue. The student wanted to say something to another student. The government, in the form of school officials, had no business trying to restrict that speech because it was not the kind of exercise of free speech that has been held to be subject to restriction, such as hate speech or incitement to imminent violence.

The case in Massachusetts demonstrated how wrong the Plano school district policy was and gave some parents there reason to believe that anti-Christian bias had to be at the bottom of the Plano policy. Even if Plano officials were themselves Christians, and even if the anti-Christian bias was not motivated by hate but by fear (of losing control of the school, for instance, as articulated by the district's attorney, who said parents wanted to use the school to proselytize), it was anti-Christian bias nonetheless.

If the Plano administrators were worried about the enormous influence of the megachurches and the rise of evangelicals, if they were worried that they might soon lose control of the school hallways to proselytizers and that they might soon lose control of the school curriculum to creationists and Christian fundamentalists, they should be informed of the attitude of evangelical leaders like Dr. Graham of nearby Prestonwood Baptist Church. "I know the assumption is that aggressive Christians are going to move into the schools and start teaching the Bible and start teaching creationism and turn the public schools into religious organizations. I don't know any responsible person who wants to do that," Dr. Graham told me.

"I'm sure there are people who want the Bible taught in public schools as literature, and I'm not a big proponent of that. The Bible's not a book of literature. It's a spiritual book, and to teach it as anything else is a problem," Dr. Graham said, taking essentially the same position as the evangelical church leader in Mustang, Oklahoma, who wanted religion taught but devotional lessons reserved for church. "I'm not an advocate of trying to go into the public schools and teach the Bible. Number one, Who's going to teach it? Is it going to be a Baptist? Is it going to be a Mormon? Is it going to be a Catholic? So the people that I run with, people in our church, nobody I know is trying to go in and take over the public schools. They just don't want to be censored and stopped and suppressed in terms of their religious freedom of speech."

As I mentioned above, there are instances where the American

Civil Liberties Union has entered disputes on the side of religionists who feel their free speech rights are being unconstitutionally restricted, but more often the ACLU is blamed as a prime player in the anti-Christmas movement and the anti-Christian bias.

The Newton County school board in Covington, Georgia, quaked in fear of the ACLU. The Mustang, Oklahoma, school superintendent, Karl Springer, made a disastrous decision to ban a nativity scene in the school play on the basis of legal advice from a lawyer worried about a letter from the ACLU. The school board in Baldwin City, Kansas, fired Santa Claus after a demand letter from the ACLU. In two of those three cases school board members were quoted as saying that the ACLU bullied and engaged in intimidation tactics.

Does the ACLU intimidate? Is it a bully?

What does the ACLU have to say about an attitude reported widely among school boards and municipal governments in America, that the ACLU is more fearsome than the U.S. Supreme Court? While the Court says Santa is a secular symbol, the ACLU says it is a religious symbol, and school boards in many communities in America find it is safer to go with the ACLU interpretation of the law than that of the U.S. Supreme Court.

If that is not bullying, what is?

I asked the man who headed the ACLU for a third of a century, Ira Glasser.

"Are you kidding? The ACLU is a 'blip on the screen' in this country," the old ACLU warrior said. "The ACLU is small. The ACLU hasn't got a tenth of the resources, for example, that the Christian Coalition has. The ACLU for most of its history is a tiny organization."

Ira Glasser may be engaging in just a bit of hyperbole, but he might also be giving us a peek into the scope of the mind-set of the people who run the ACLU, and who believe the government (a school board, for instance) is always a Goliath and the lawyer who comes to right a wrong (from the local chapter of the ACLU) is always the little guy. Glasser led the national American Civil Liberties Union and, separately, the New York chapter of the ACLU for thirty-four years. He retired recently, in 2001, but remains as intellectually active as ever, and always ready to defend both civil liberties and the ACLU.

Trained as a mathematics professor, Glasser turned out to be one of the most eloquent and articulate (and, by the way, charming) defenders of the ACLU that the organization has ever had. Glasser is a not a lawyer, and has never been to law school, but his grasp of the law is as clear and firm as any lawyer's, and his rhetorical skills were honed by debating ACLU policies with the organization's fiercest critics, the wildly argumentative members of its own board of directors.

The ACLU's principal players today—President Nadine Strossen, Executive Director Anthony Romero, and the southern California executive director Ramona Ripston—refused to speak to me for this book. This triumverate of liberal activism was unwilling to submit to interviews to explain themselves when it became clear that the point of view of the author was that they are constricting rights and freedoms, not defending them.

But not everybody in the ACLU is so afraid of answering questions.

Glasser agreed to see me for an extended interview* to be used

*Copyright Fox News Channel.

for a television special on the ACLU that the Fox News Channel was considering producing. We argued for over two hours, and Glasser was nearly always satisfied that he had prevailed. He is an excellent debater, and he knows the subject—the ACLU—probably better than any of his critics.

I asked him about the ACLU's bullying tactics. "A school board is worried about busing, they are worried about paying teachers. The ACLU comes in . . . ," I said.

"No, they are not, " Glasser interrupted without waiting, shaking his head, rejecting the very premise of the question before he had heard it completely.

Gibson: The ACLU comes in and says, "Do what we want you to do or we are going to take money out of your budget."

Glasser: No. The ACLU never said that. And you cannot find a single instance where the ACLU has ever said that. You cannot find a letter. You cannot find a phone call. You cannot find anybody who says that the ACLU said that. You are making it up.

Glasser ignores for the convenience of his argument that an ACLU threat of litigation, even implied, always carries with it the certainty that the ACLU will ask to recover costs, and if it prevails, judges will grant the ACLU attorney fees in the many thousands of dollars.

"Now, what the ACLU does say . . . ," Glasser started to go on, trying to move away from a point he didn't like, but I interrupted again.

Gibson: You think I am not going to be able to find a letter that says that? . . .

Glasser: No.

Gibson: . . . that the ACLU said, "If you don't stop this practice . . ."

Glasser: Now wait a minute.

Gibson: ". . . we are going to sue."

Glasser: Now you are switching ground.

Gibson: No, I am not.

Glasser: Yes, you are.

Gibson: That's exactly what I am talking about.

Glasser: Read the transcripts. First you said that you think the ACLU comes in and says, "If you don't do what we want we are going to take your money." And I said, "The ACLU never said that." Then you backtracked, and you said, "You don't think I am going to be able to find a letter where the ACLU says, 'If you don't stop practice X, we are going to sue you.'" Oh yeah, the ACLU would send that letter. Yes. Right.

Gibson: "And we are going to take your money. We are going to recover our costs"?

Glasser: I doubt you will ever find a letter that says, "We are going to recover our costs."

But the ACLU refrains from saying explicitly only what is certain to be understood implicitly.

After all, that was exactly the threat in Baldwin City, Kansas, and in Covington, Georgia, that made the school boards in those places fire Santa Claus and expunge the word "Christmas" from the school calendar. When the ACLU contacted Karl Springer in Mustang, Oklahoma, about the nativity scene in the school pageant, Springer was immediately worried about the solvency of his district.

The ACLU, Glasser said, goes after schools "that use the government's tax-raised money to impose somebody else's religious views on children and their families who don't share those views." He doesn't mention that the ACLU sometimes tries to enforce a ban on "religious views" (Christmas trees, Santa Claus, the singing of Christmas carols) that the Supreme Court of the United States has ruled permissible.

(Glasser had said earlier in the interview that the ACLU has never been wrong, but it has occasionally been "prematurely right." When the ACLU argues on an issue the Court has already decided, the ACLU merely takes the position that it is ahead of the crowd again.)

Gibson: Do you believe Santa Claus is a *religious* symbol?

Glasser: I didn't see it growing up as a Jew, I'll tell you that much.

Gibson (incredulous): In New York City, you never saw Santa Claus?

Glasser: Not as a Jew.

Gibson: The *Miracle on 34th Street*? The movie about Santa Claus set in New York City considered a Christmas season classic. You didn't see that?

Glasser: You have no idea, the isolated community I grew up in.

(Not so isolated that Glasser didn't meet and marry a Christian woman.)

Gibson: You really believe that Santa Claus is not a secular symbol?

(Santa is secular, by the way, is the precise position of the United States Supreme Court.)

Glasser: Santa Claus is *not* a secular symbol. Santa Claus comes out of the Christian tradition. And if you don't think so, you are living on another planet from me. Not to mention the fact that I don't think the ACLU ever sued a school board about Santa Claus. It sued school boards about nativity scenes.

Glasser is being slippery about that, of course, unless he means that no lawsuit was required after the ACLU lawyer made officials back down with a simple letter. The school board in Baldwin City, Kansas, of course, was not sued, but it did receive a letter from the ACLU threatening to sue if the board did not cease the practice of sending their Santa Claus to visit elementary schools. And Glasser was evidently unaware of the ACLU's actions in Covington, Georgia.

ACLU critic Bill Donohue of the Catholic League has referred to ACLU thinking in his books as "atomistic." It is hard to understand what Donohue means until you argue with a man like Ira Glasser. Atomistic is another way of saying "hairsplitting." Can I find a case where the ACLU sued over Santa Claus? That isn't the point, is it? The ACLU, with the threat of using its legal muscle to win and then ask the judge to award legal fees, seldom has to actually sue. Mostly all it has to do is send a letter, a threat, and the school board backs down, feeling threatened, feeling bullied, feeling intimidated.

What did Glasser say when a school board feels that way? "Good. Because if they didn't feel that way they would have gone ahead. They were restrained."

Glasser insisted that the ACLU does not have a political agenda, but it is without question a liberal, if not leftist, organization. Once again, with their atomistic view of argument, I have no doubt Glasser and other ACLU officials would contest the point, but I believe it is a purely observational matter that is indisputable. ACLU members, staff, donors, its leadership are liberal and left wing. It is true that the ACLU defended Oliver North and William F. Buckley, Jr., on purely free speech grounds, and it should have done so in both cases. But that does not detract from any claim that the organization's people—staff and donors—are predominantly liberals and bring a liberal, leftist point of view to much of their analysis of rights in our society.

And if Glasser and the others at the ACLU are worried that their religious rights, sometimes described as "freedom FROM religion," are under attack, they are correct.

A growing number of Christians feel that it is wrong for their religion to be treated as something people should be protected from.

The rise of the Christian legal organizations means that the ACLU lawyer in small-town America is not going to be able to simply roll over a school board or a city manager and impose by threat a policy that exceeds the parameters enunciated by the United States Supreme Court. Because there are Christian litigators around the country willing to take on these cases, Ira Glasser's view that Santa Claus is a religious symbol is now no longer likely to trump the U.S. Supreme Court's view that it is not.

While the ACLU, the Americans United for Separation of Church and State, and the Anti-Defamation League have had a relatively free hand to pursue anti-Christmas policies that are essentially anti-Christian, and while they have had success in suppressing Christianity illegally and unconstitutionally, those days are coming to a close, thanks to the efforts of thousands of lawyers who have risen up and said, "We're mad as *heck* [some might say "hell"] and we're not going to take it anymore."

It is also a warning for all those officials in positions of petty ministerial power in this country that casually stepping on the rights of Christians to have their religious holiday, Christmas, appear in public is not going to go unchallenged.

In Plano, Texas, the school board had taken the position that in maintaining neutrality between people of faith and people of nonfaith, nonfaith became defined as the neutral position. So in this competition for space in the public square, the religionists had lost, and the nonreligionists were victorious right from the first day. After all, what do the people of nonfaith want? They want religion out of the schools completely.

What was created in Plano, where even red and green were banned, was a concept of separation of church and state that had turned into an official hostility to religion—at least in the judgment of a group of parents who filed a lawsuit. If even the presence of certain colors which represent Christmas at that time of the year was too much to be permissible, then the message is that religion is wrong, it is in error, it is flawed, it is not worthy, it is an embarrassment. That message constitutes a prohibition of the free expression of that religion, and that is plainly unconstitutional.

What I have learned is that Christmas is the new litmus test of the nation's willingness to abide by its own Constitution, to make certain people are free to express their religion without being told that they must keep their beliefs private and tucked out of sight.

I have also learned about what one of the Christian lawyers referred to as the "offended observer." If the standard of admission to the public square is whether anyone from any background with any point of view is offended by any minor, even insignificant, symbol of Christmas and Christianity, then Christmas and Christianity always lose. There is always somebody to gripe, to complain, to feel resentful, to object, and if the mere act of objecting carries the day, then Christmas and Christians always lose.

Any situation designed for one party to always lose will always engender resentment and resistance.

Which is precisely where we are today. The revolution against Christianity has been under way for a few years, and now the counterrevolution is gearing up.

Those who would ban Christmas and Christians should not mistake the signs on the horizon. The Christians are coming to retake their place in the public square, and the most natural battleground in this war is Christmas.

The war on Christmas is joined.